Magnificent Mandalas

Mandala Coloring Book

*50 Adult Coloring Book Stress Relieving
Patterns Volume 2*

Lone Star Coloring

Magnificent Mandalas Volume 2

Is a collection of 50 highly detailed Mandala images. One image per page. The images are suitable for adults and older children. These images are perfect for gel pens, color markers, fine tip color pens and color pencils.

Lone Star Coloring is committed to bringing you the most beautiful adult coloring books in the universe. Coloring time gives you the ability to relax, decompress and unstress. Rediscover the art of coloring. We would love for you to share your colorings. Please post them to Facebook.com/LoneStarColoring. Rediscover the art of coloring. Relax and enjoy!

LoneStarColoring.com
Dallas, Texas

Relax and Have Fun Coloring!

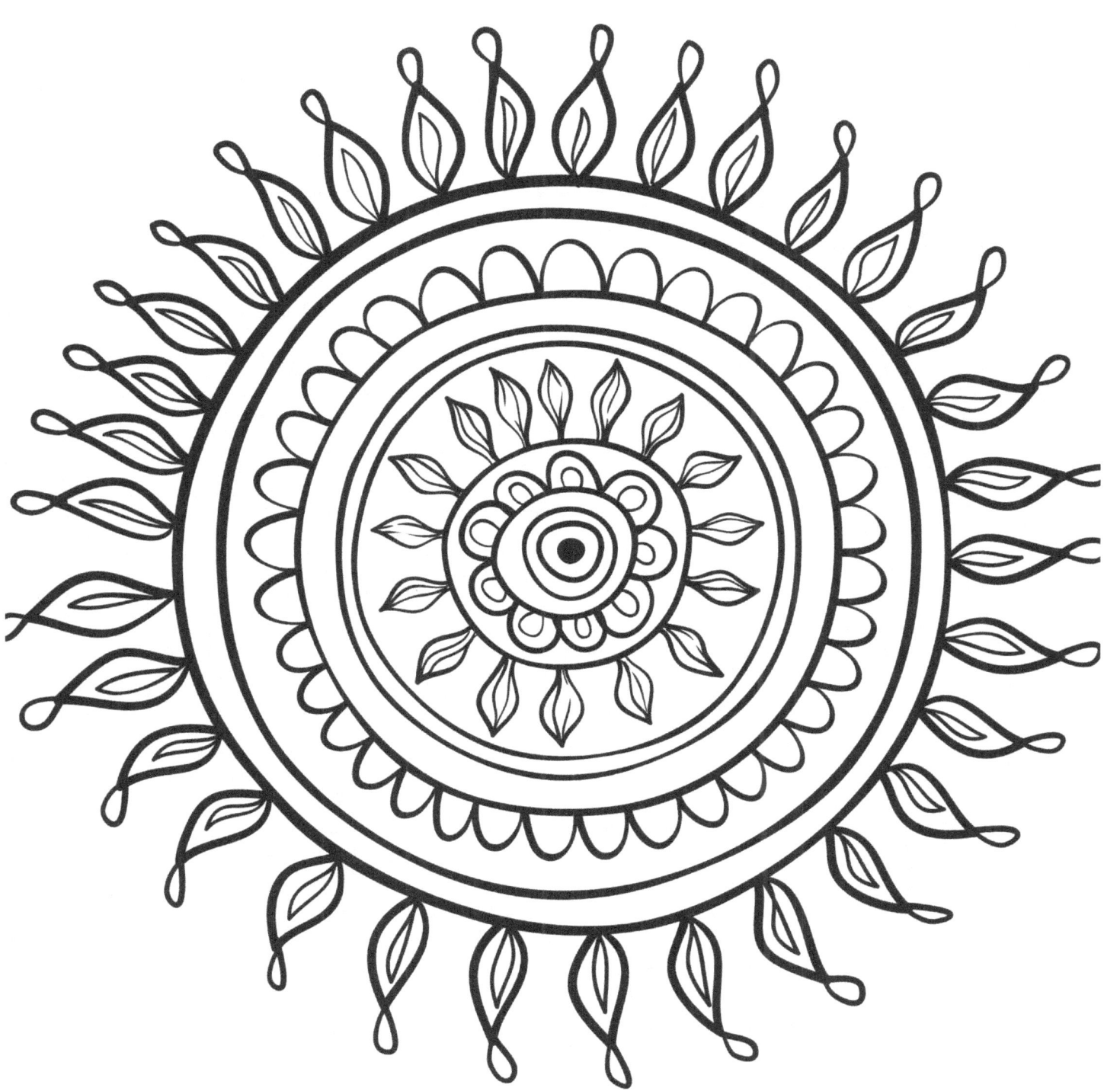

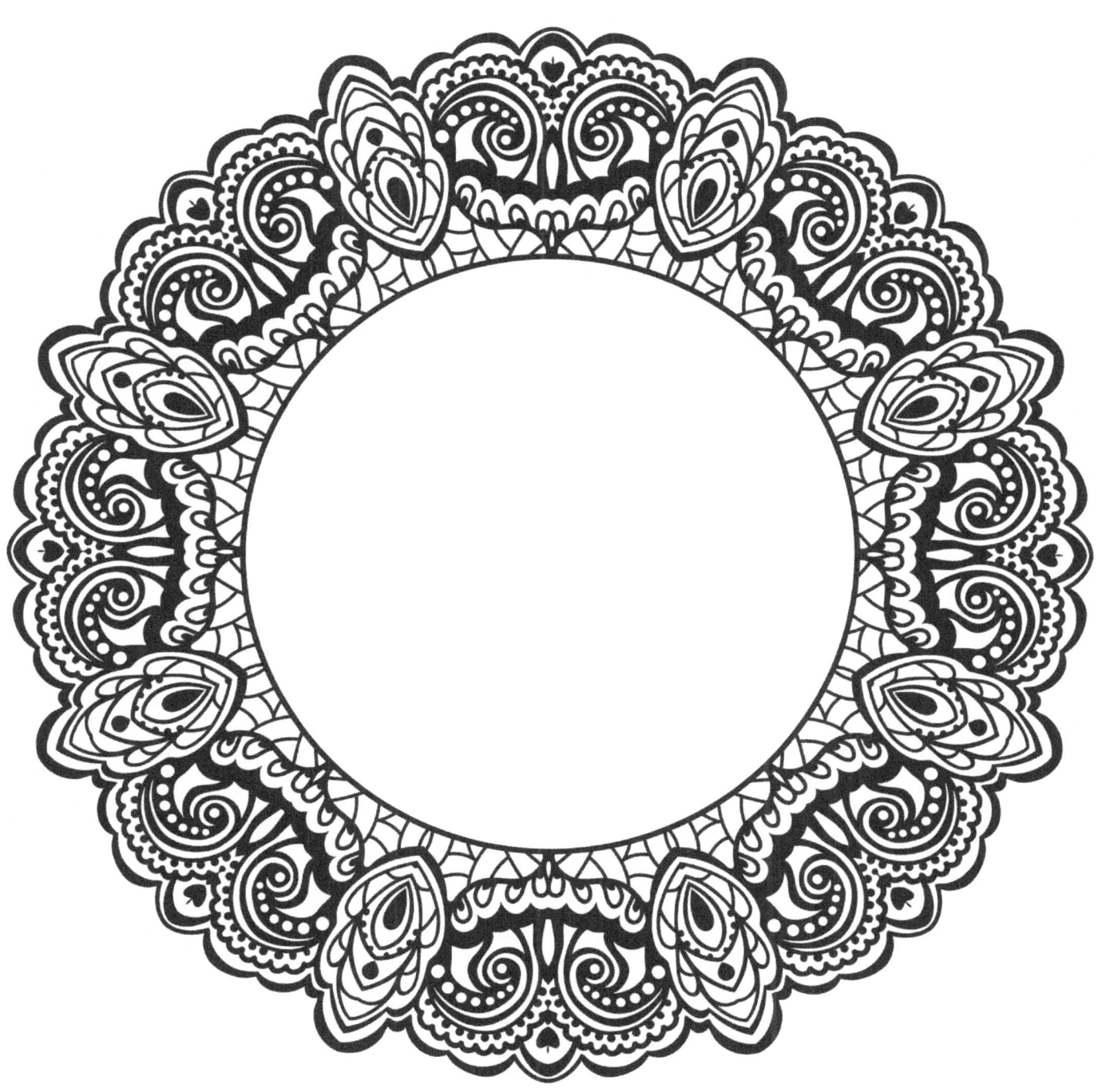

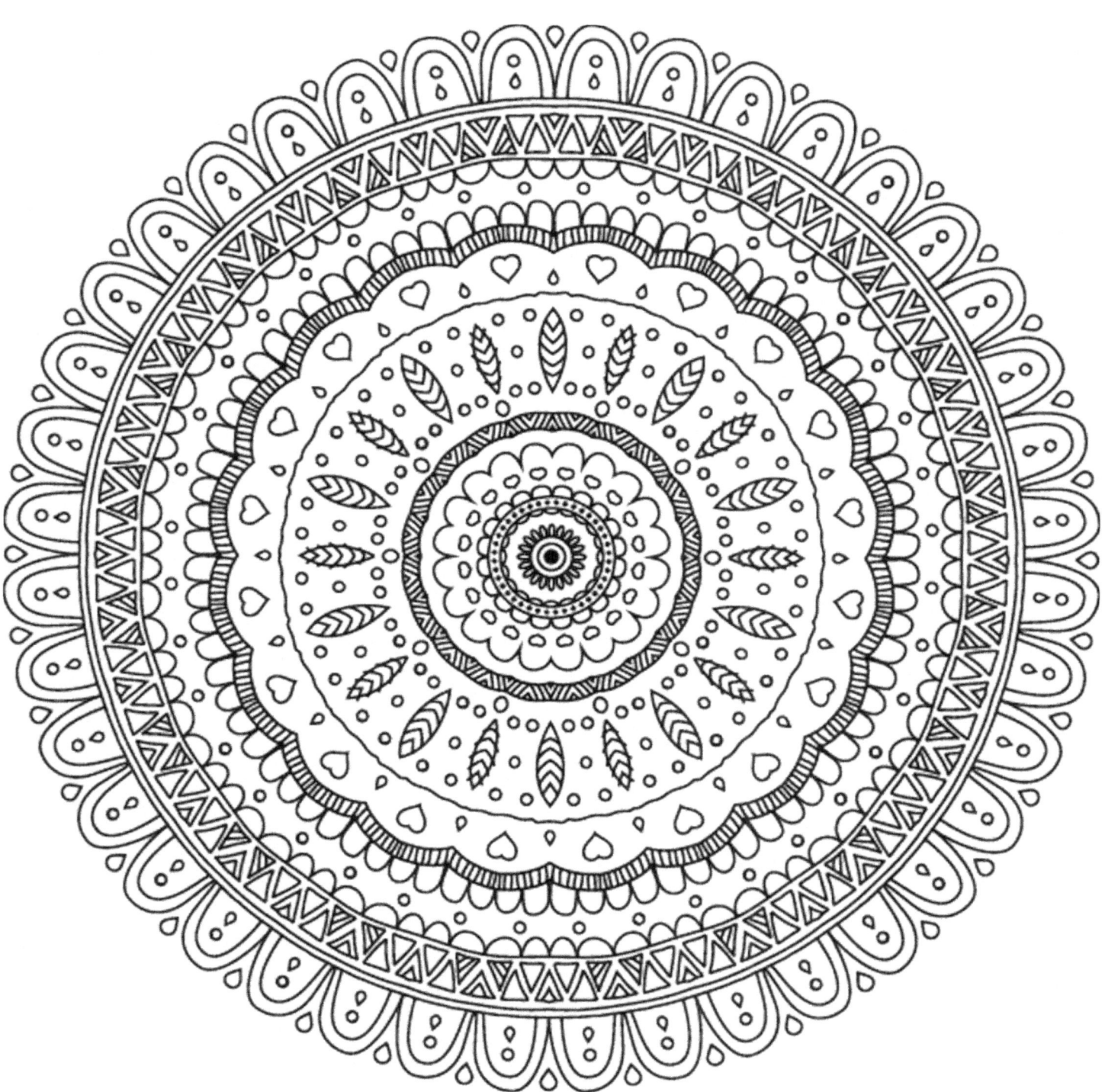

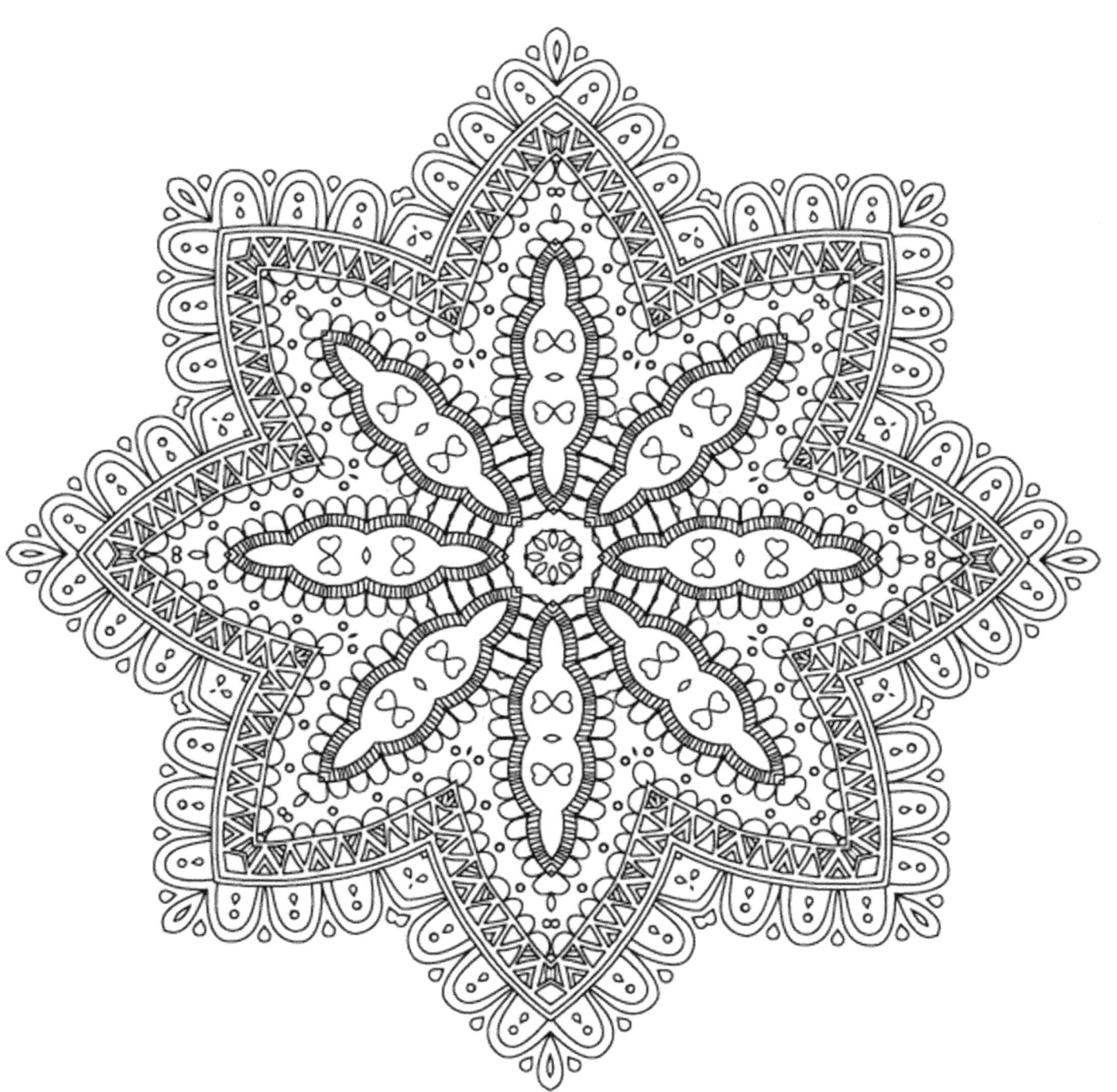

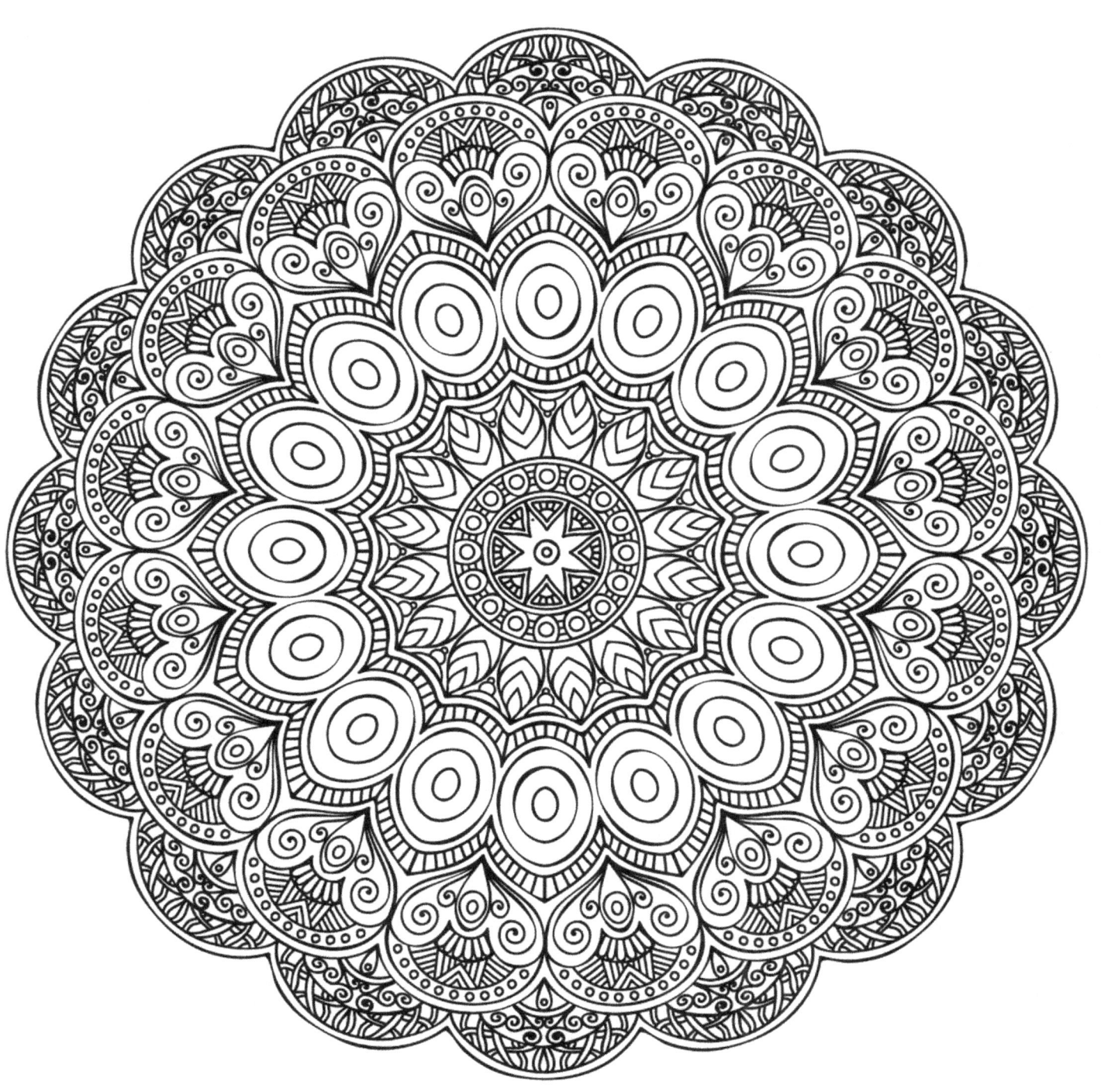

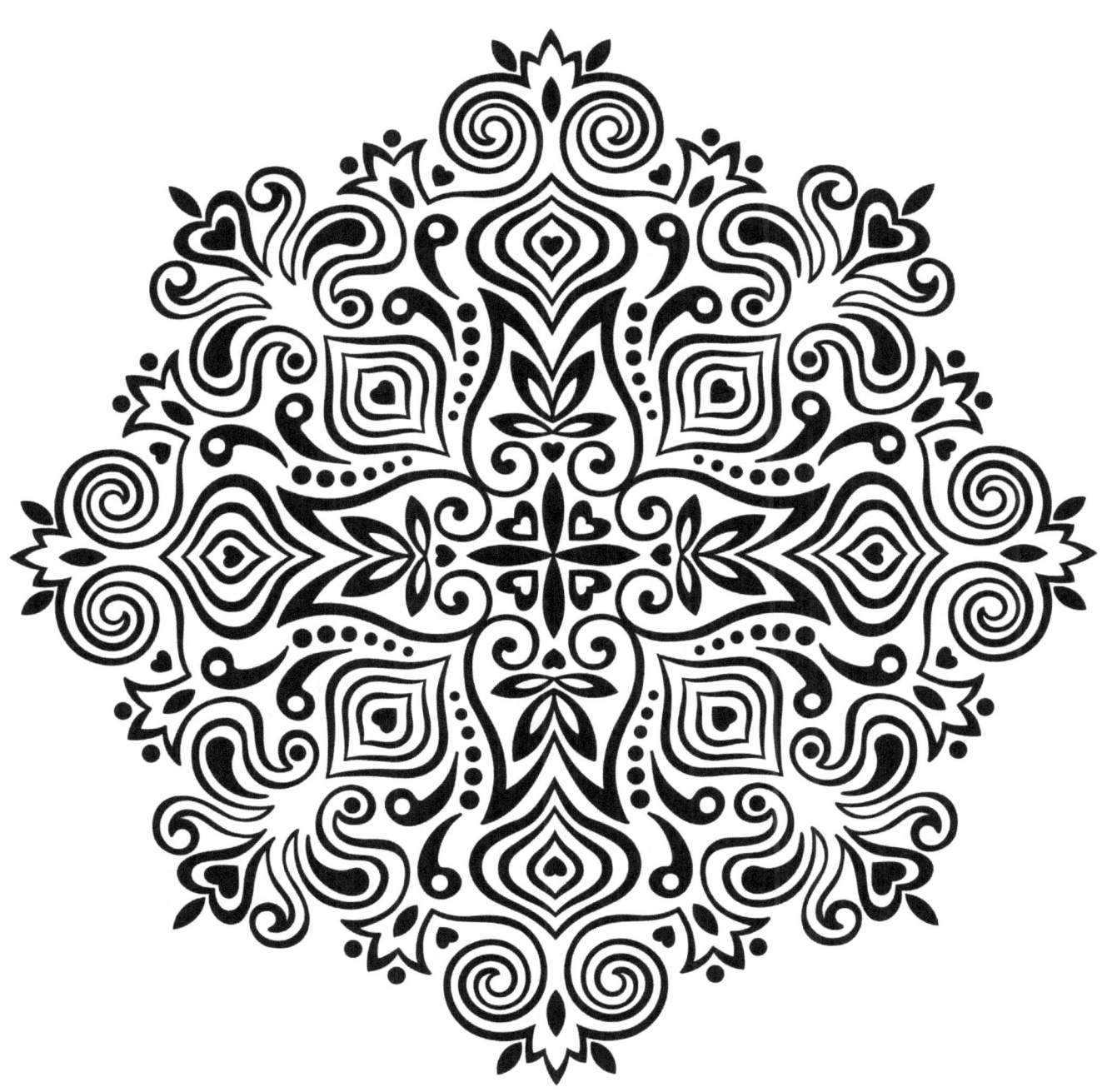

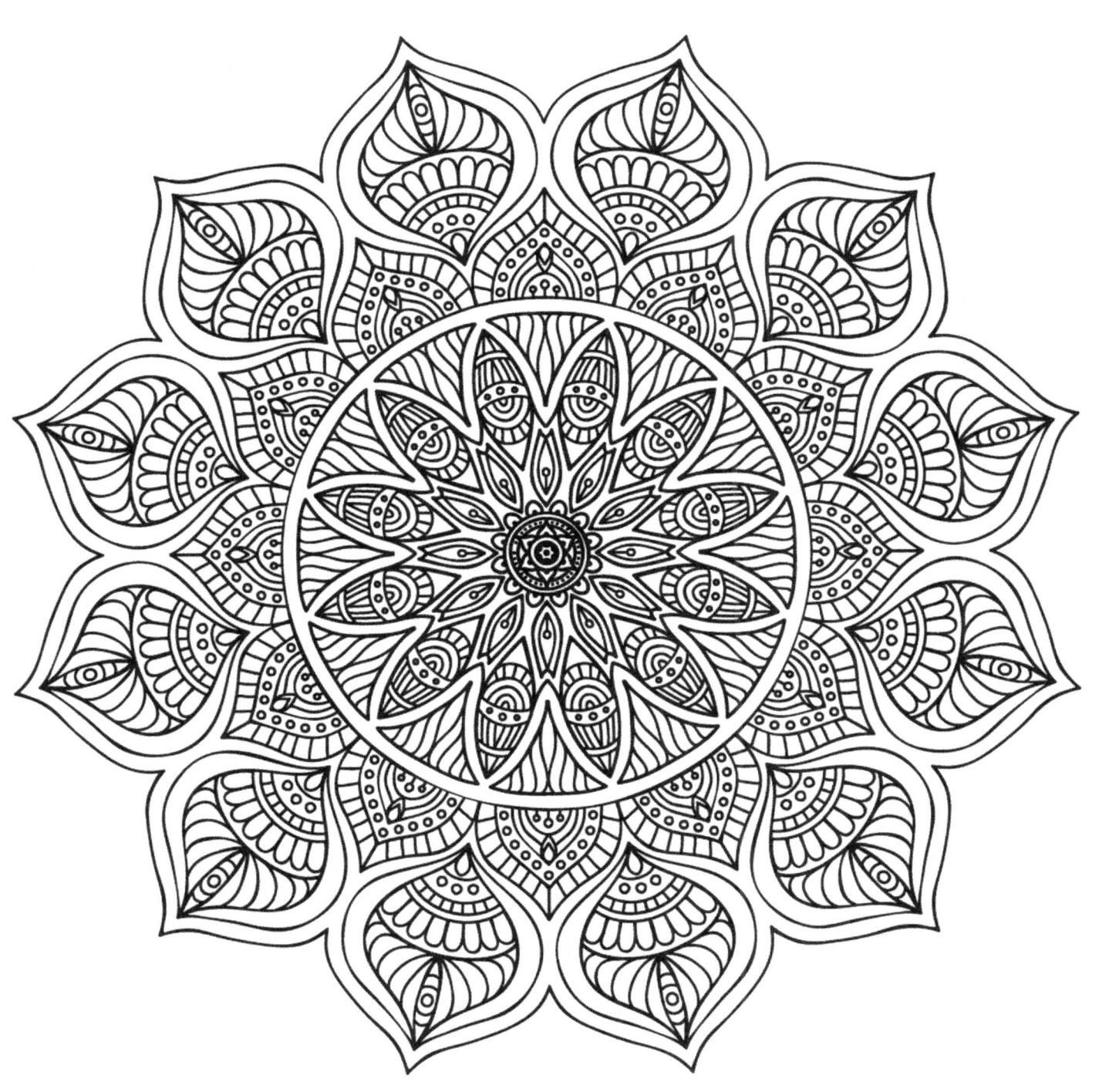

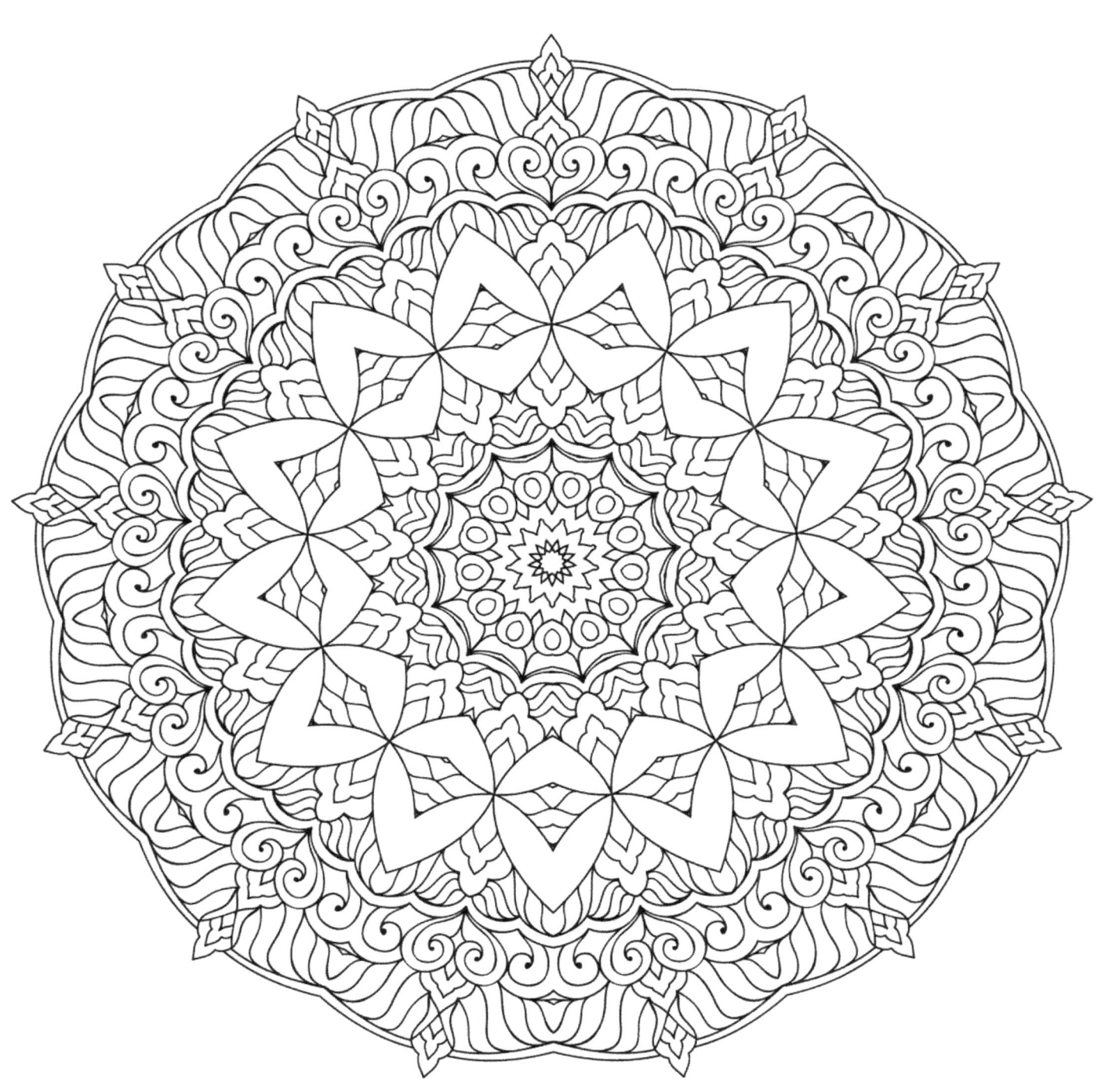

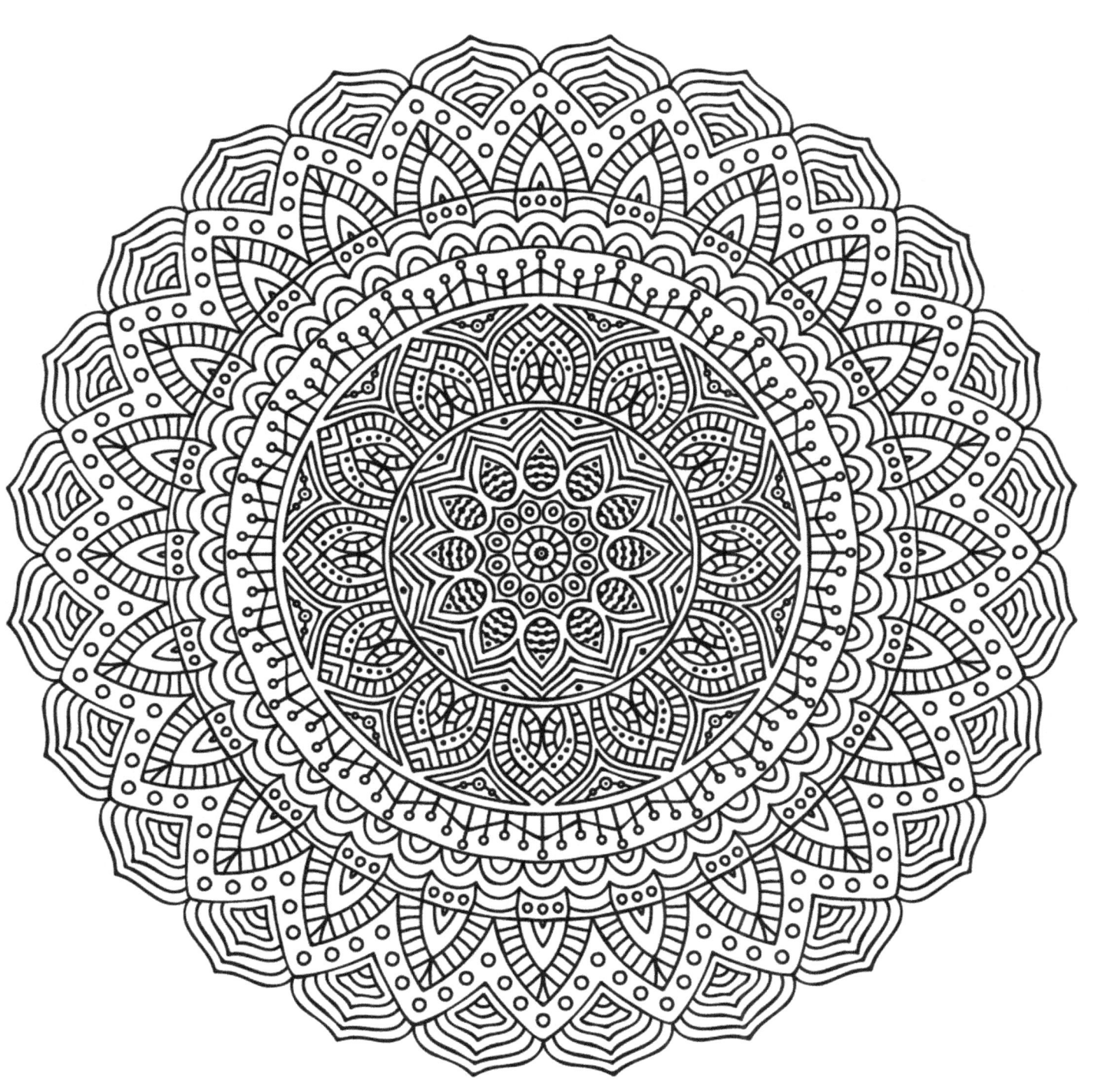

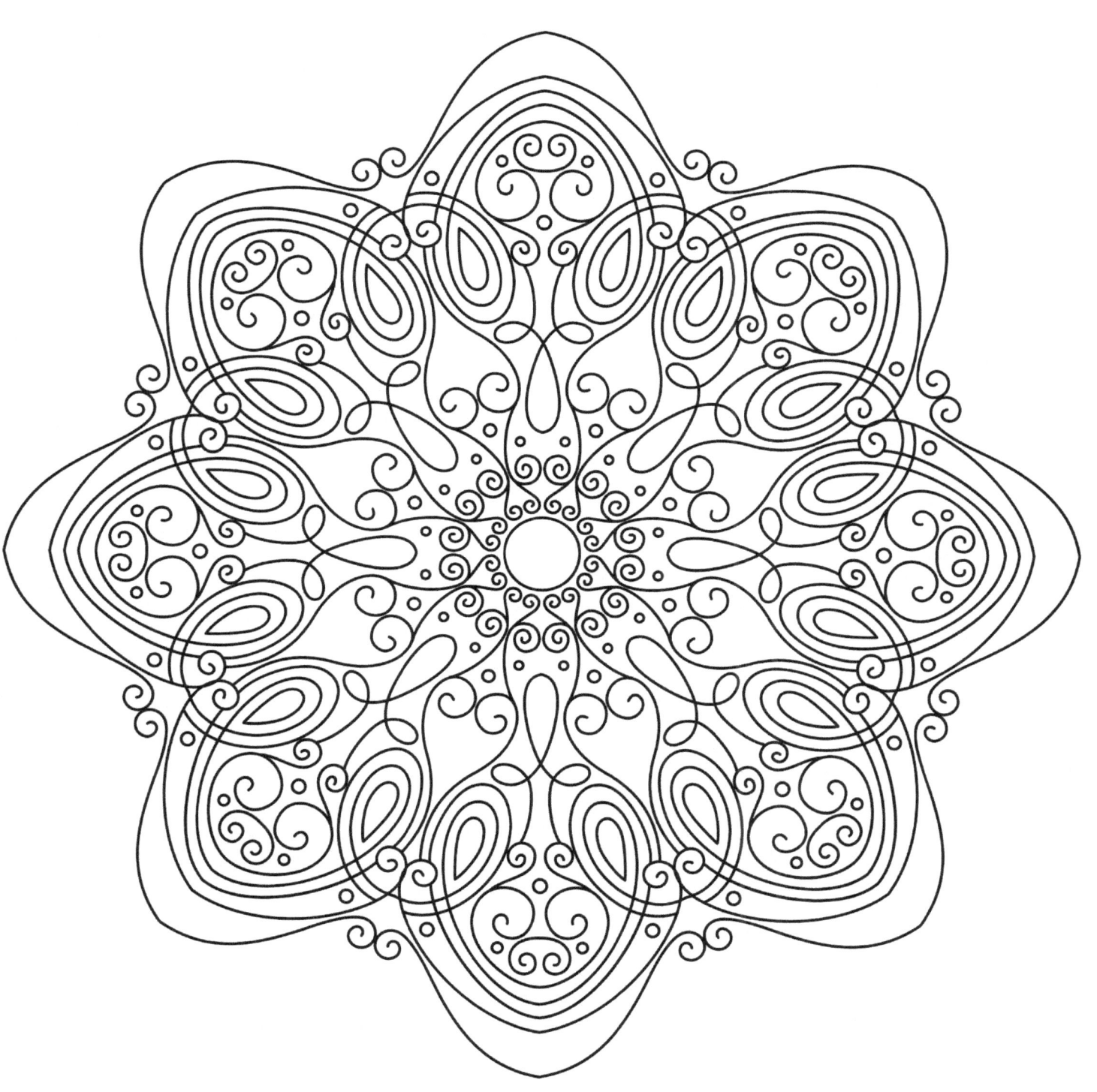

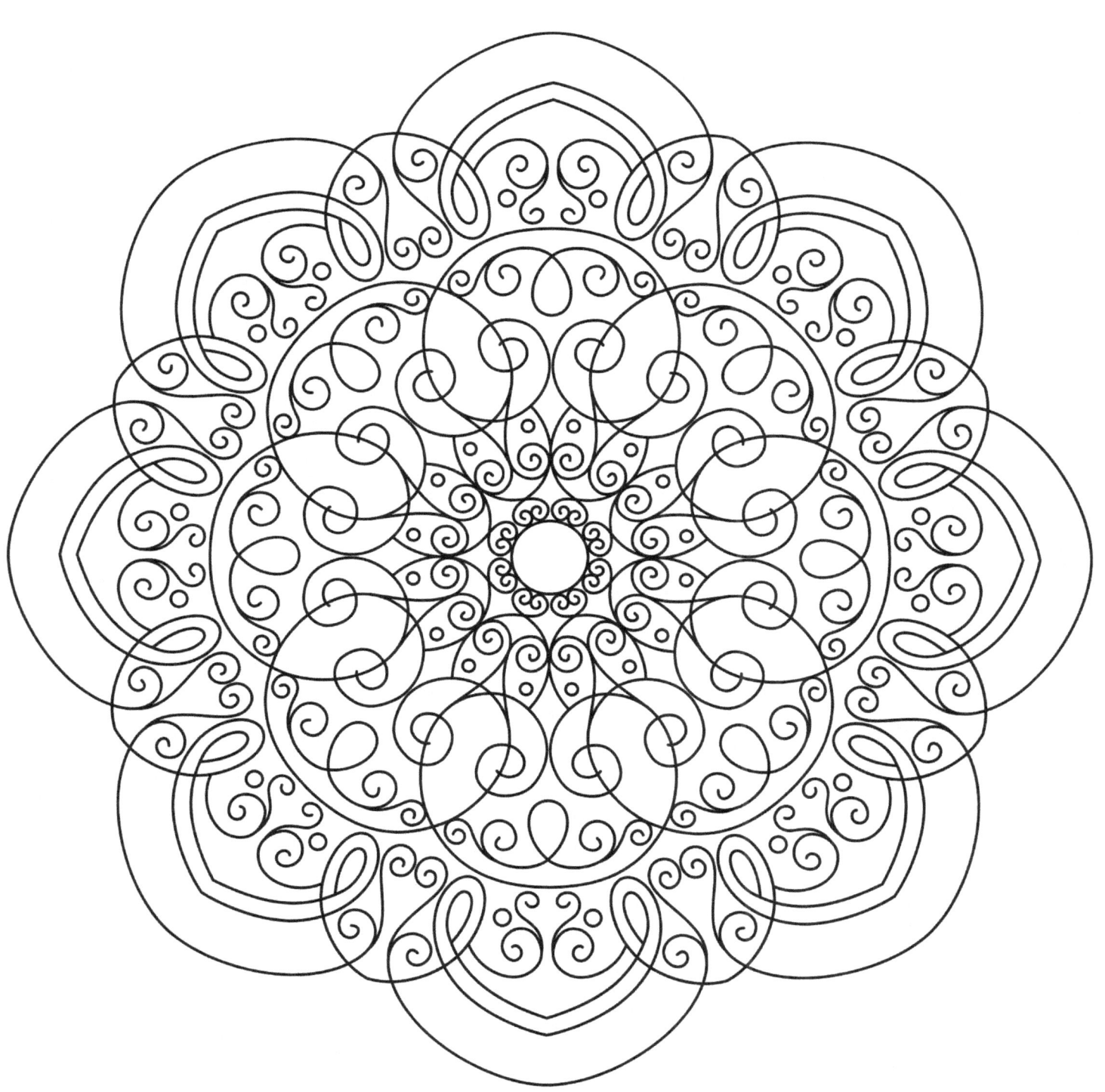

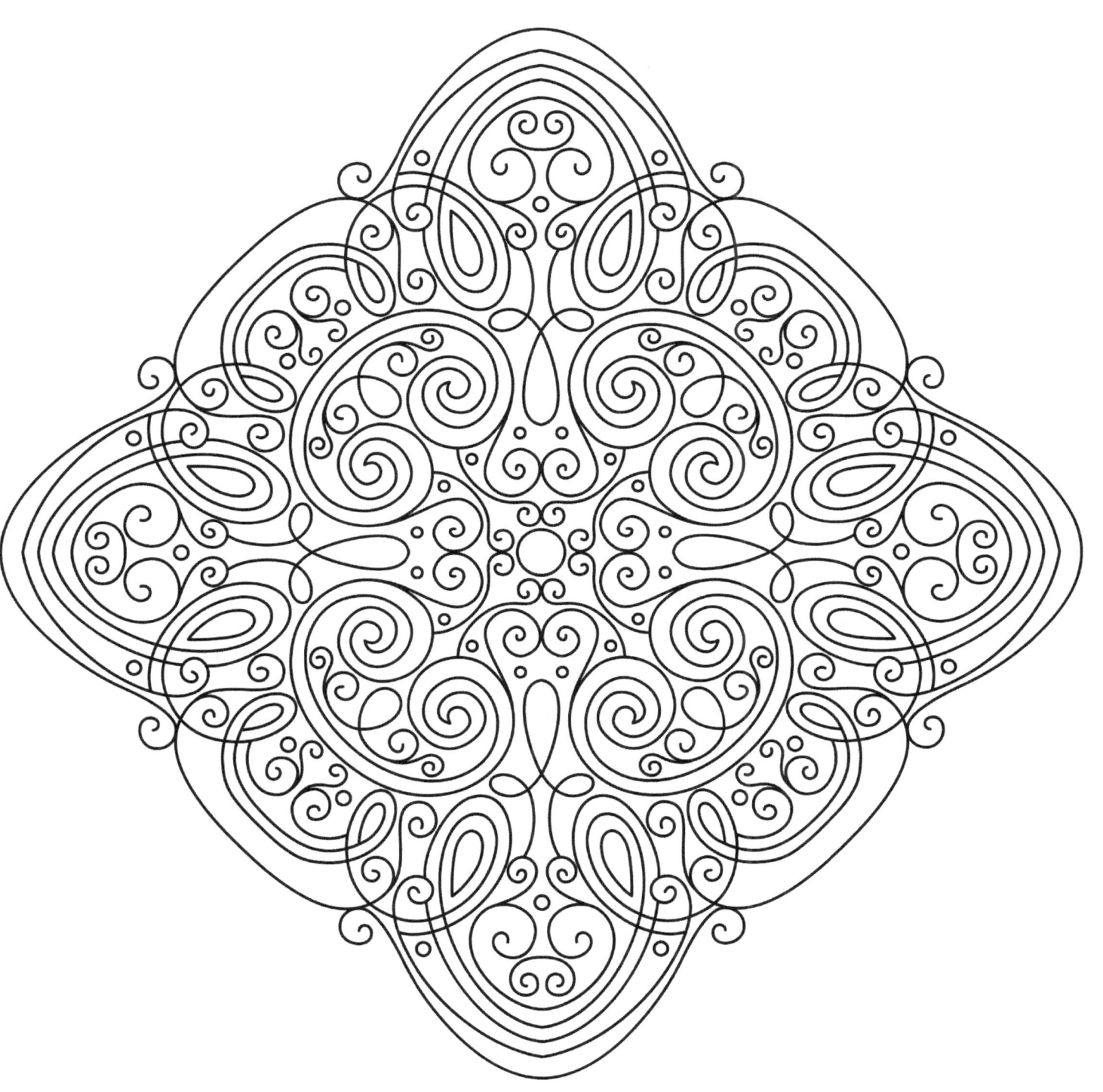

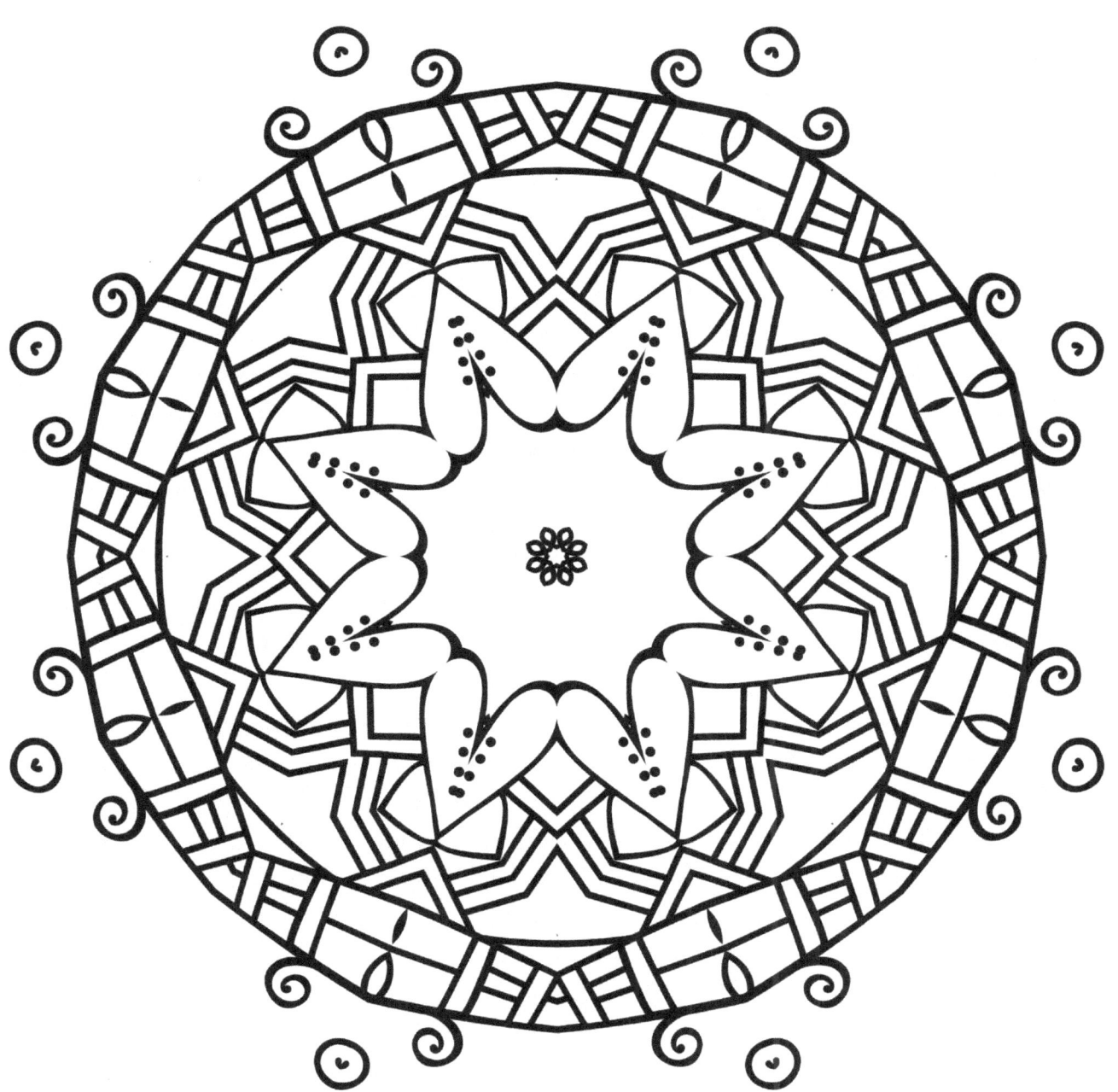

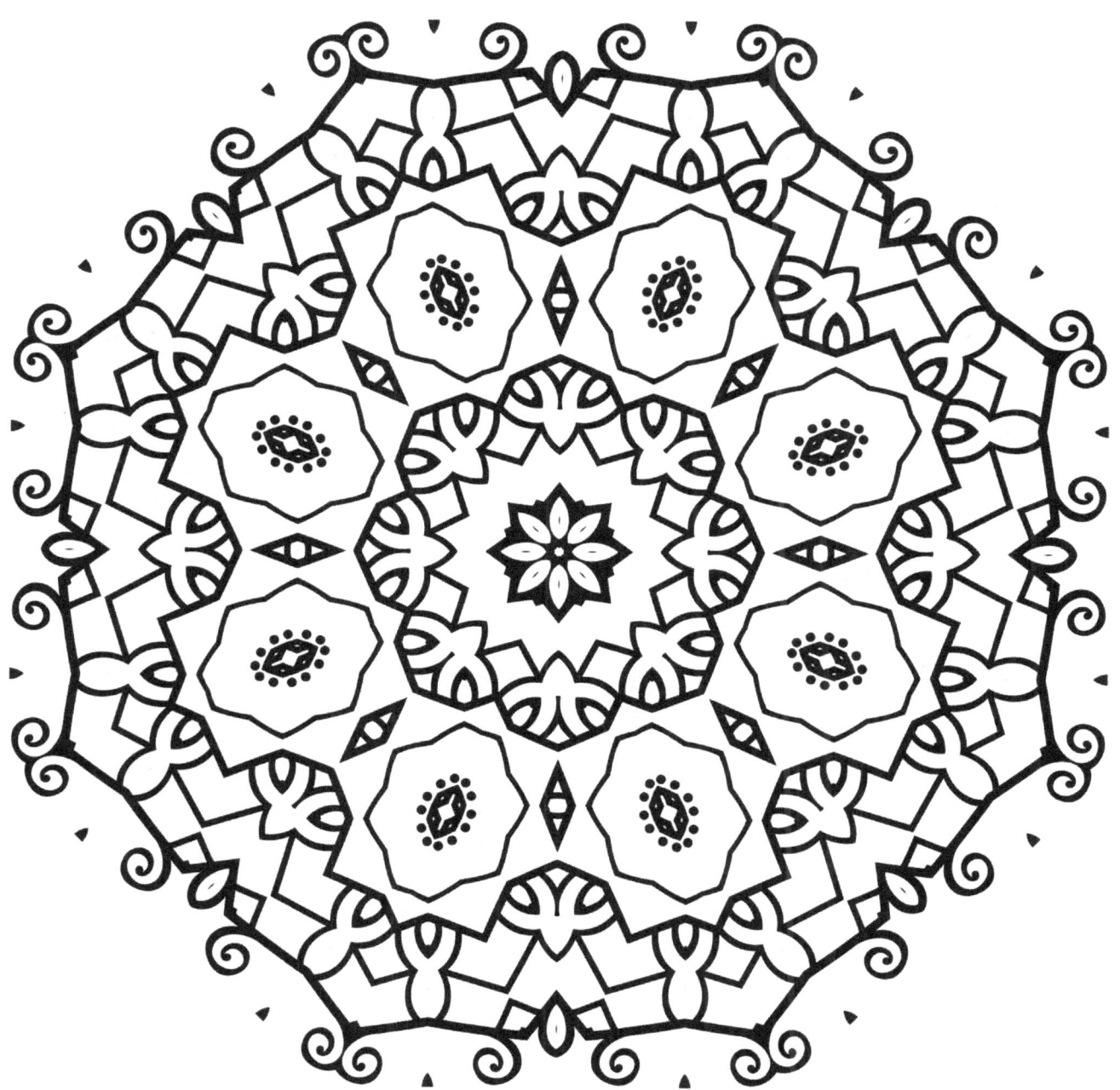

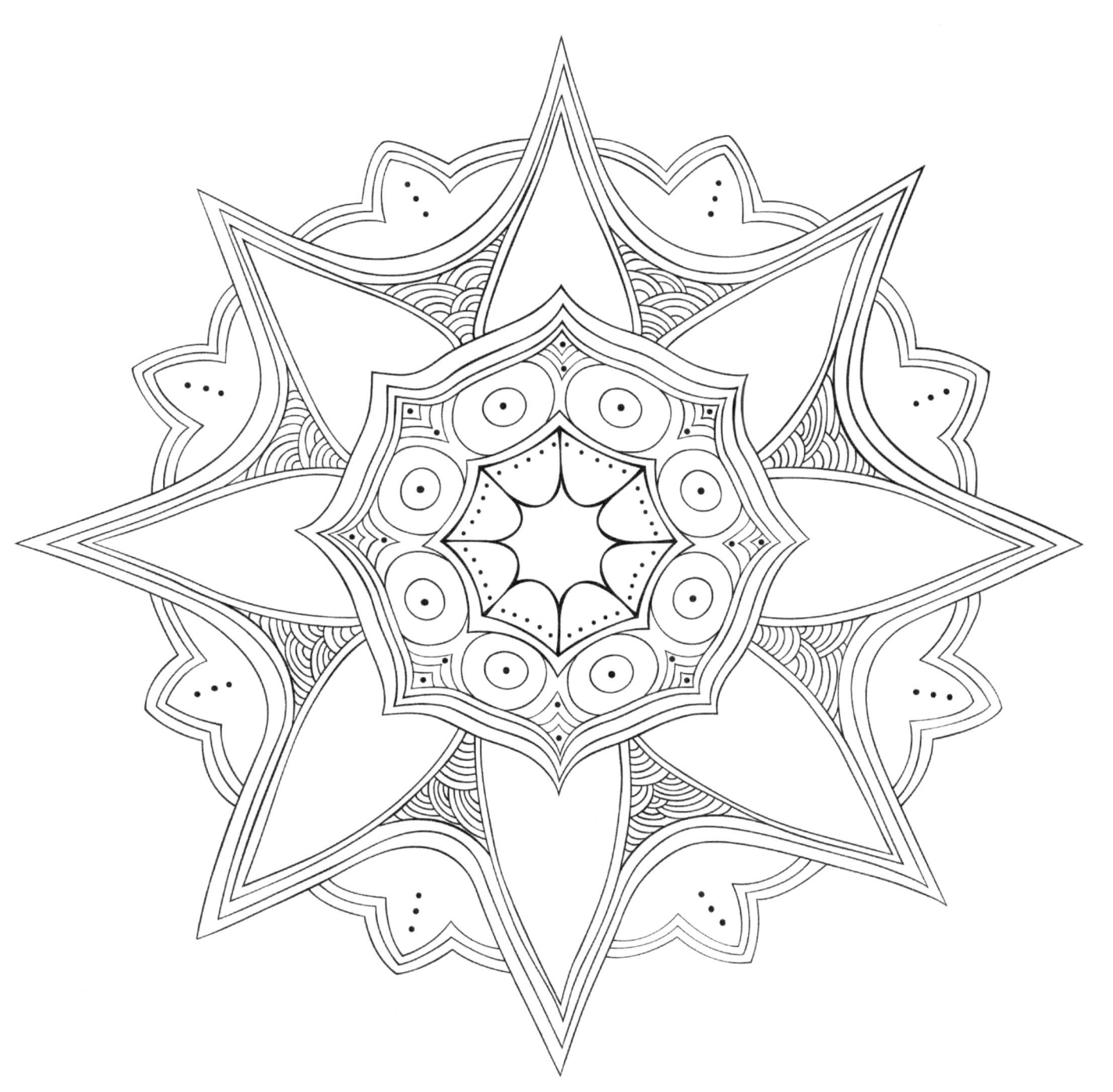

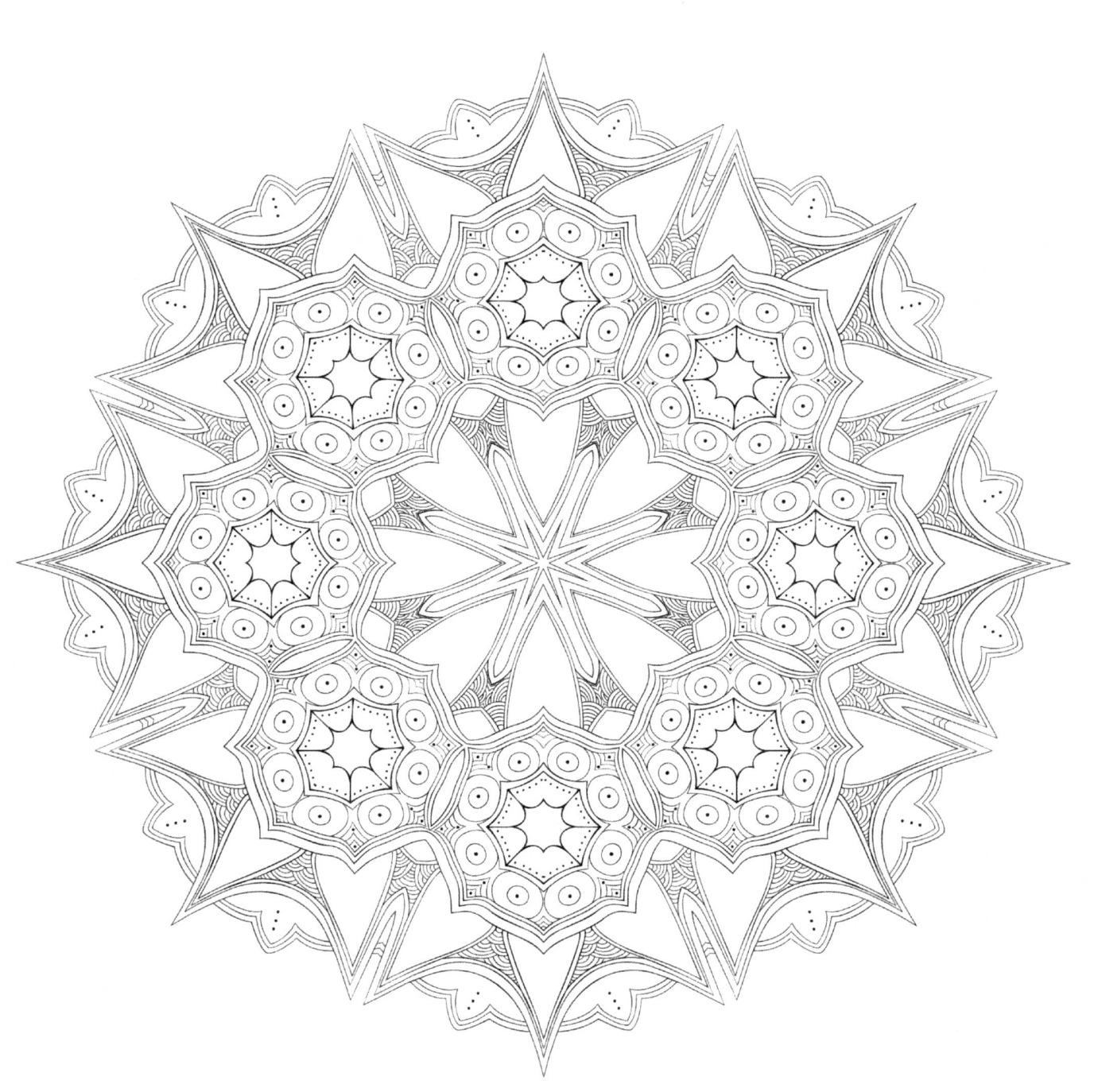

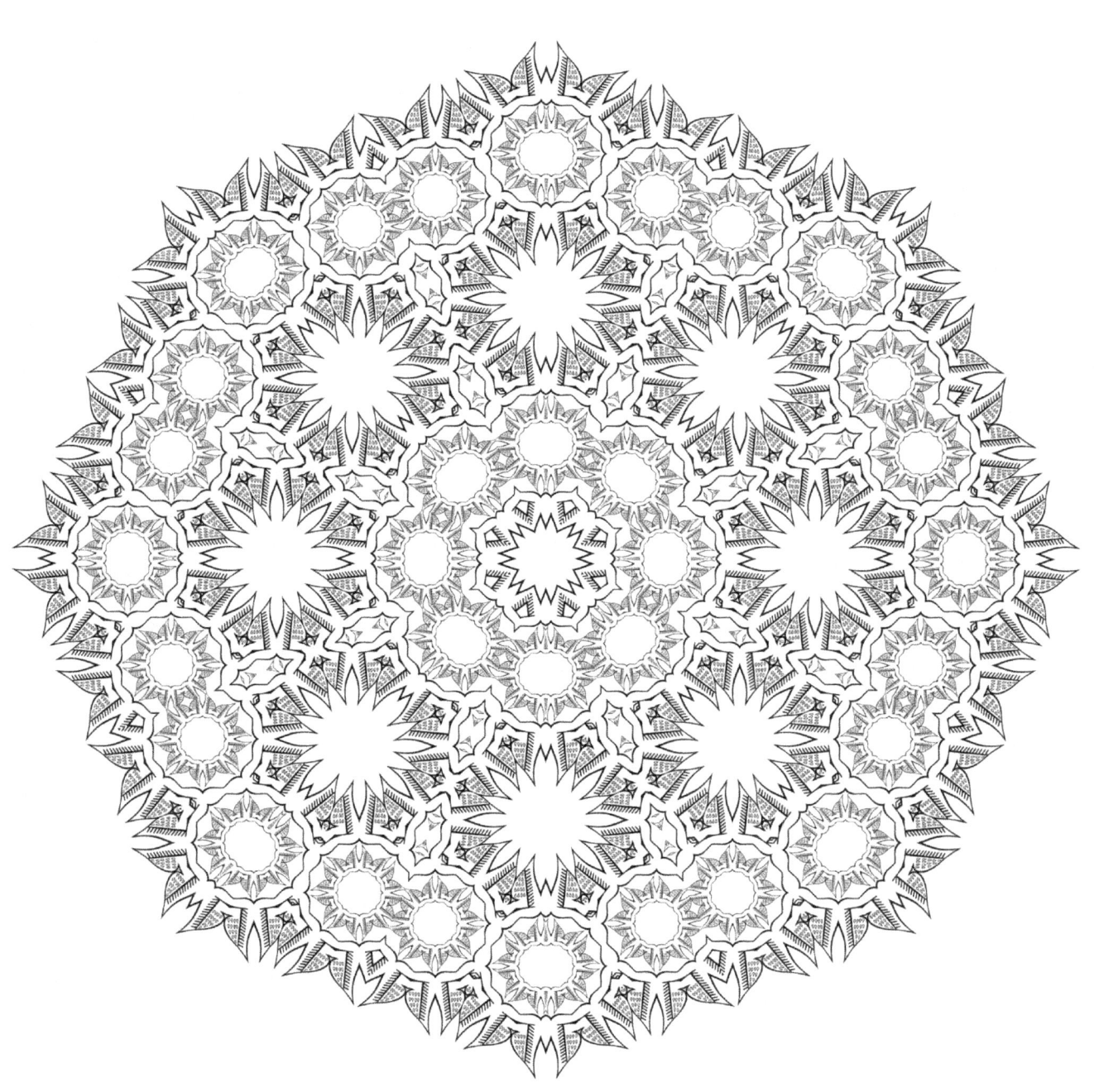

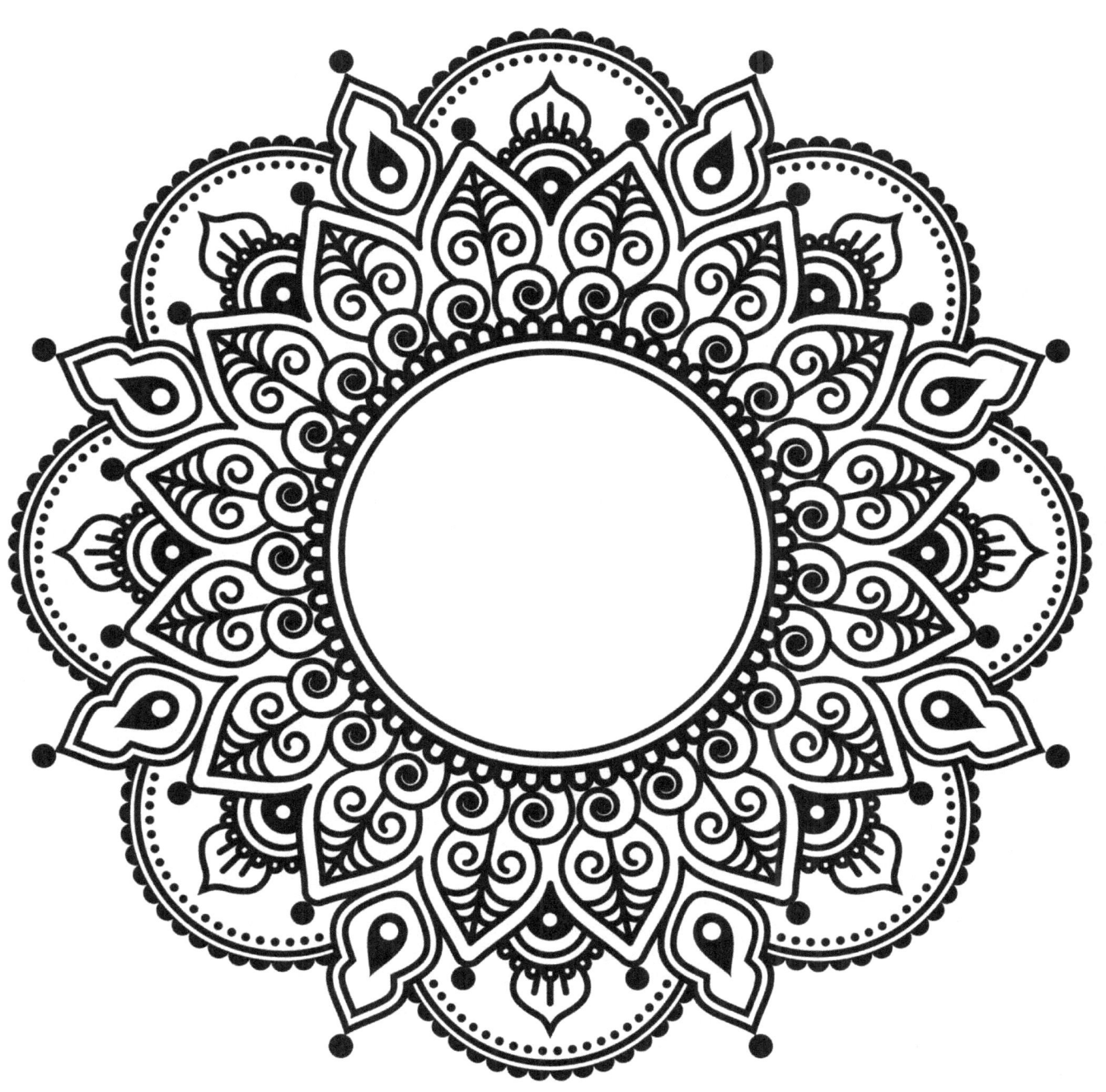

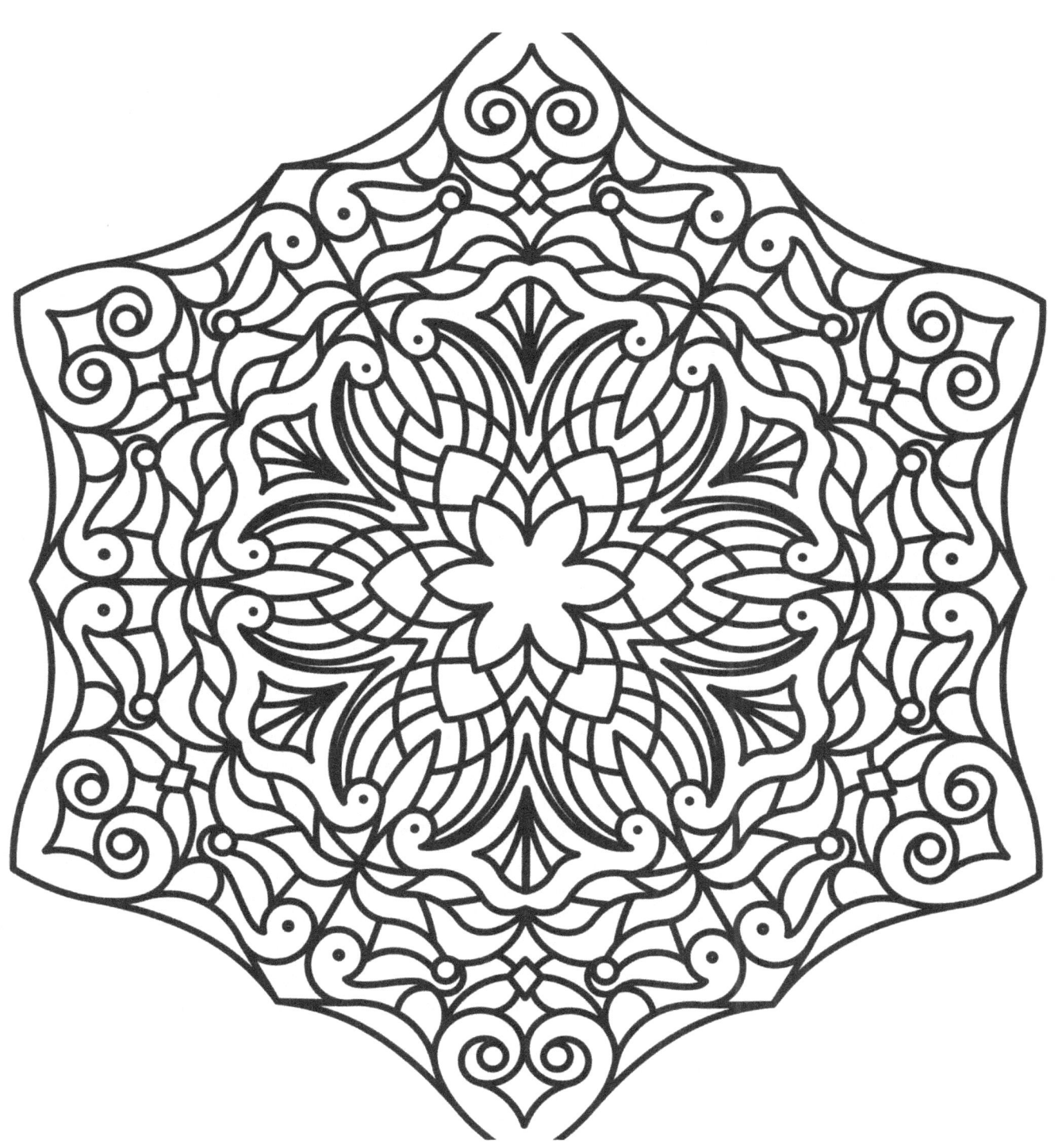

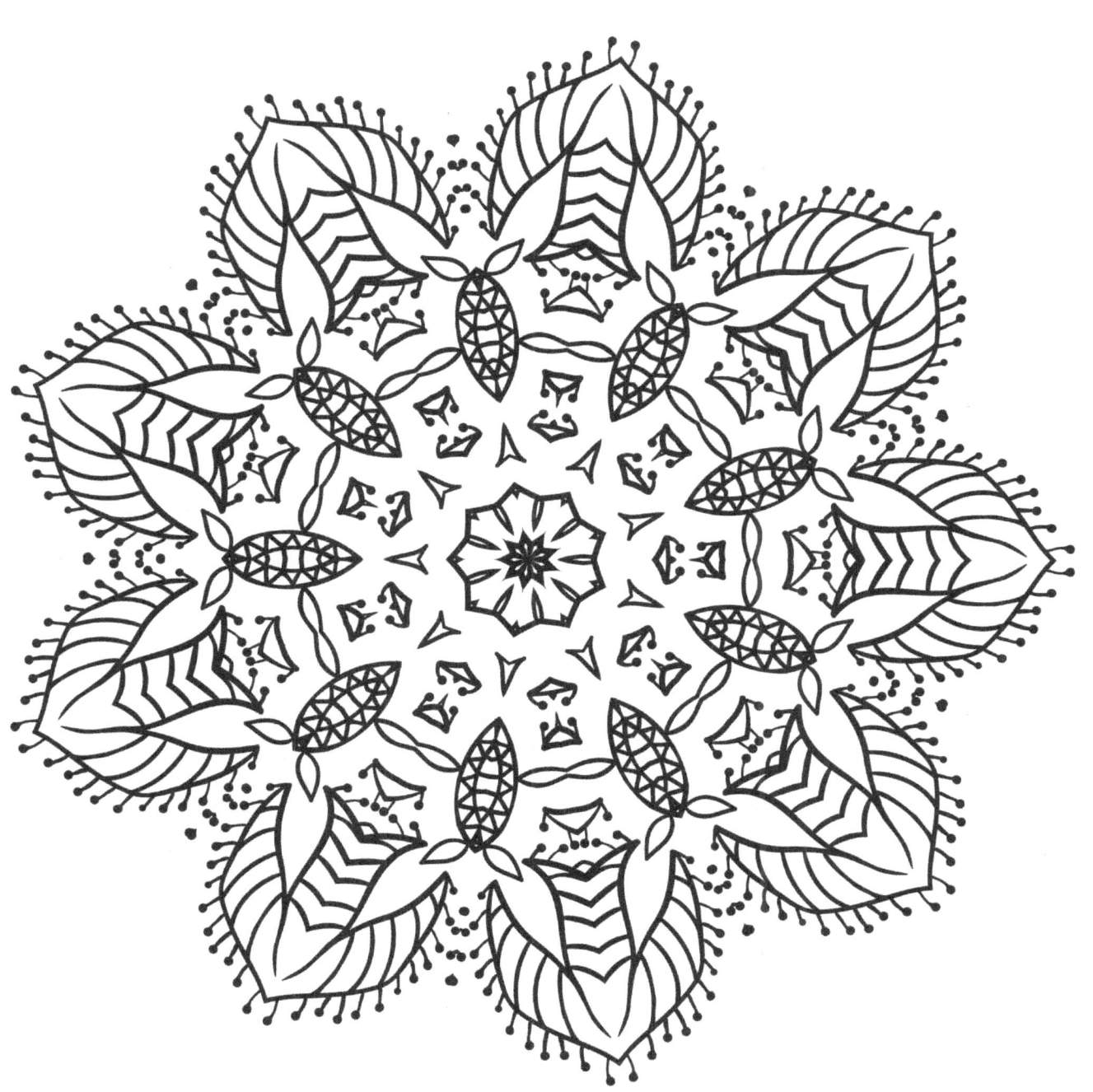

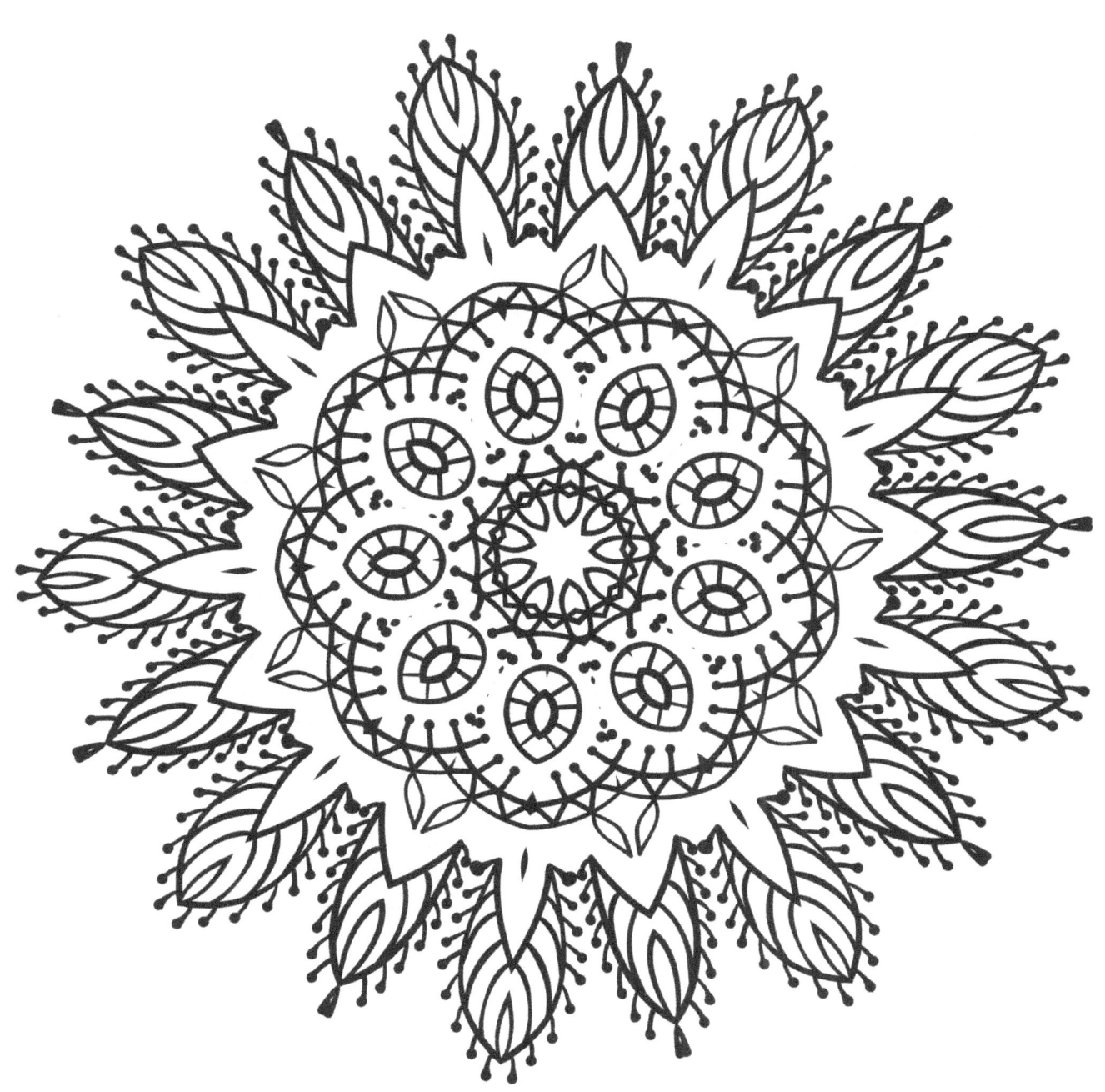

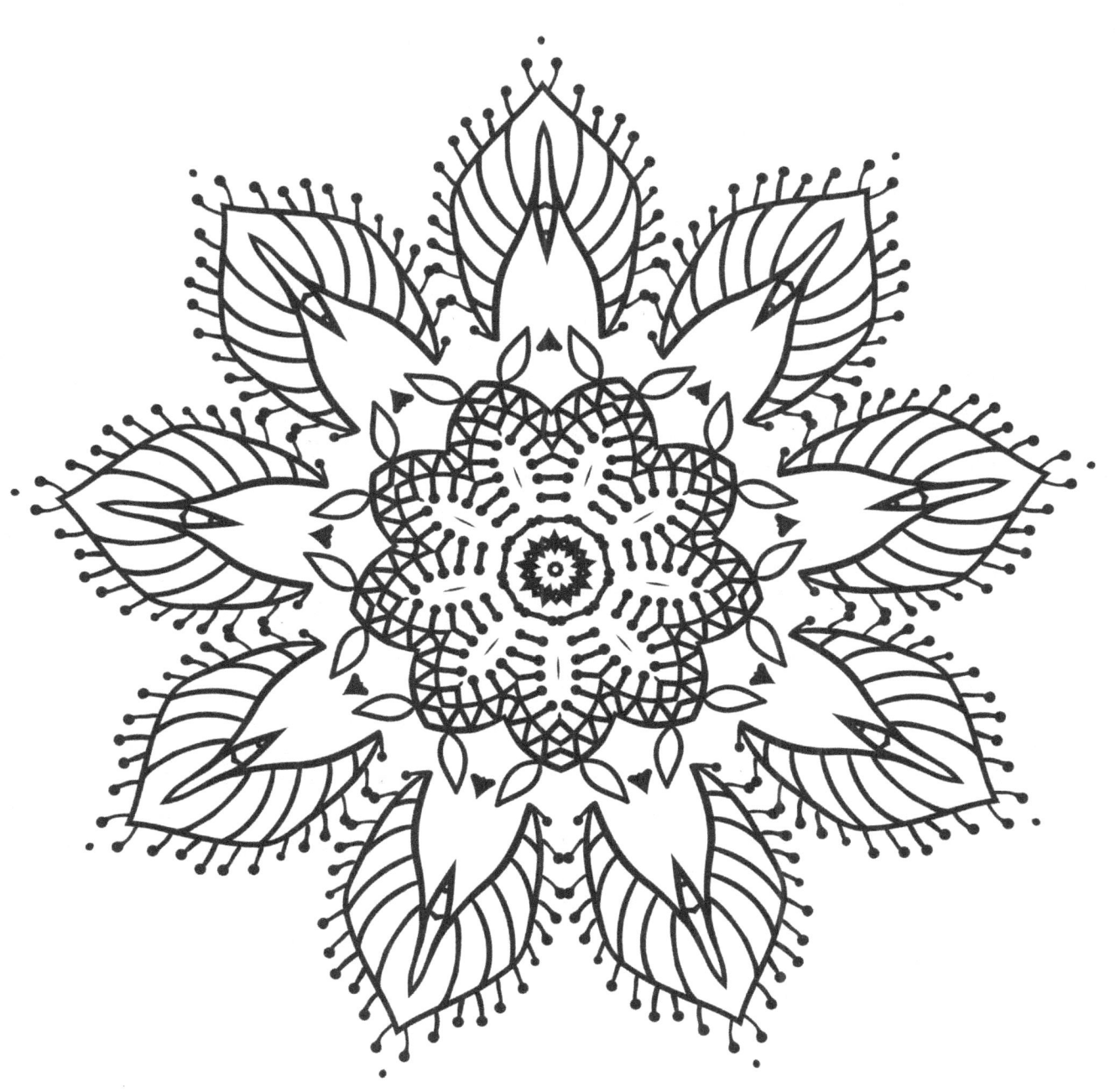

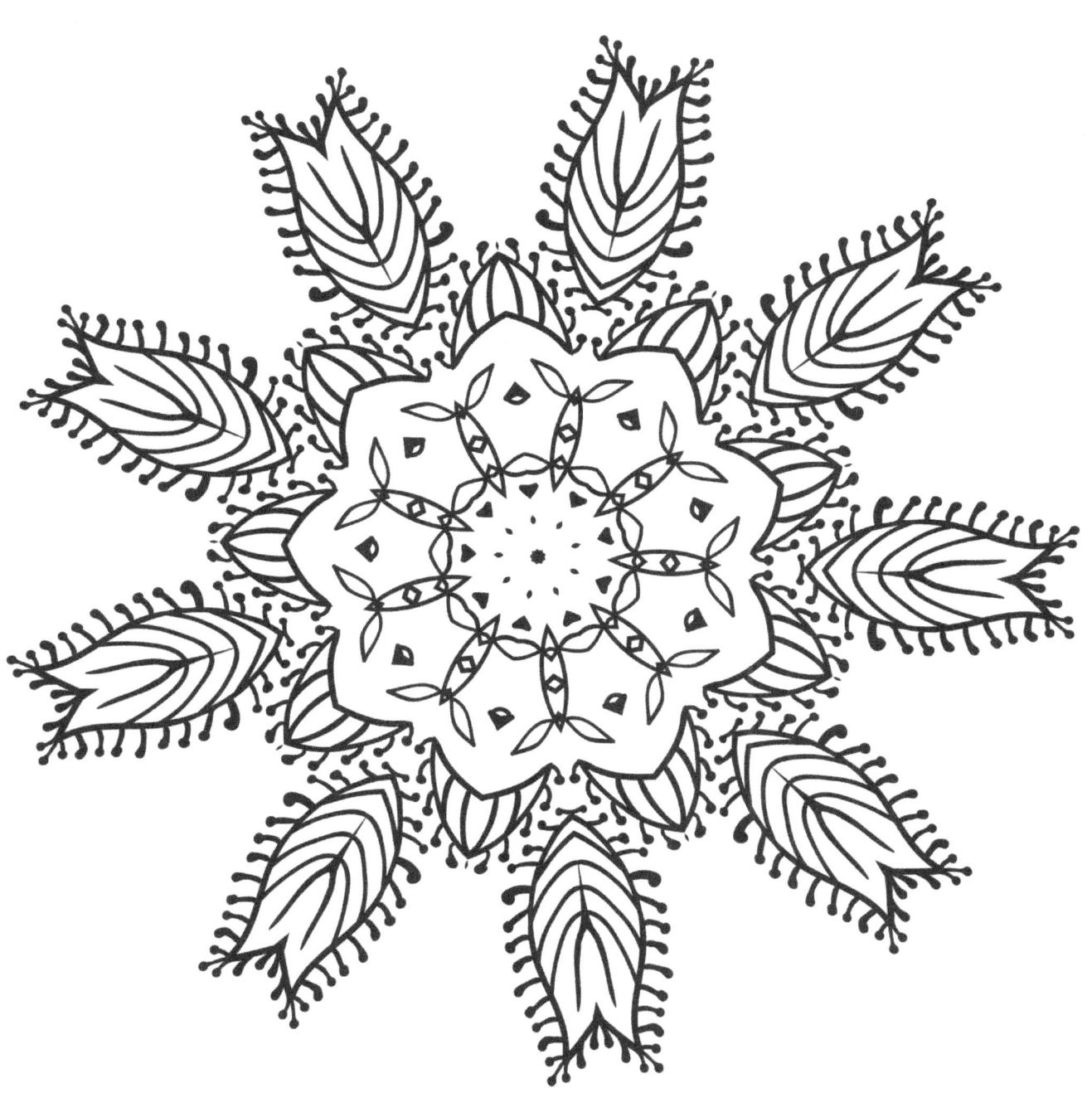

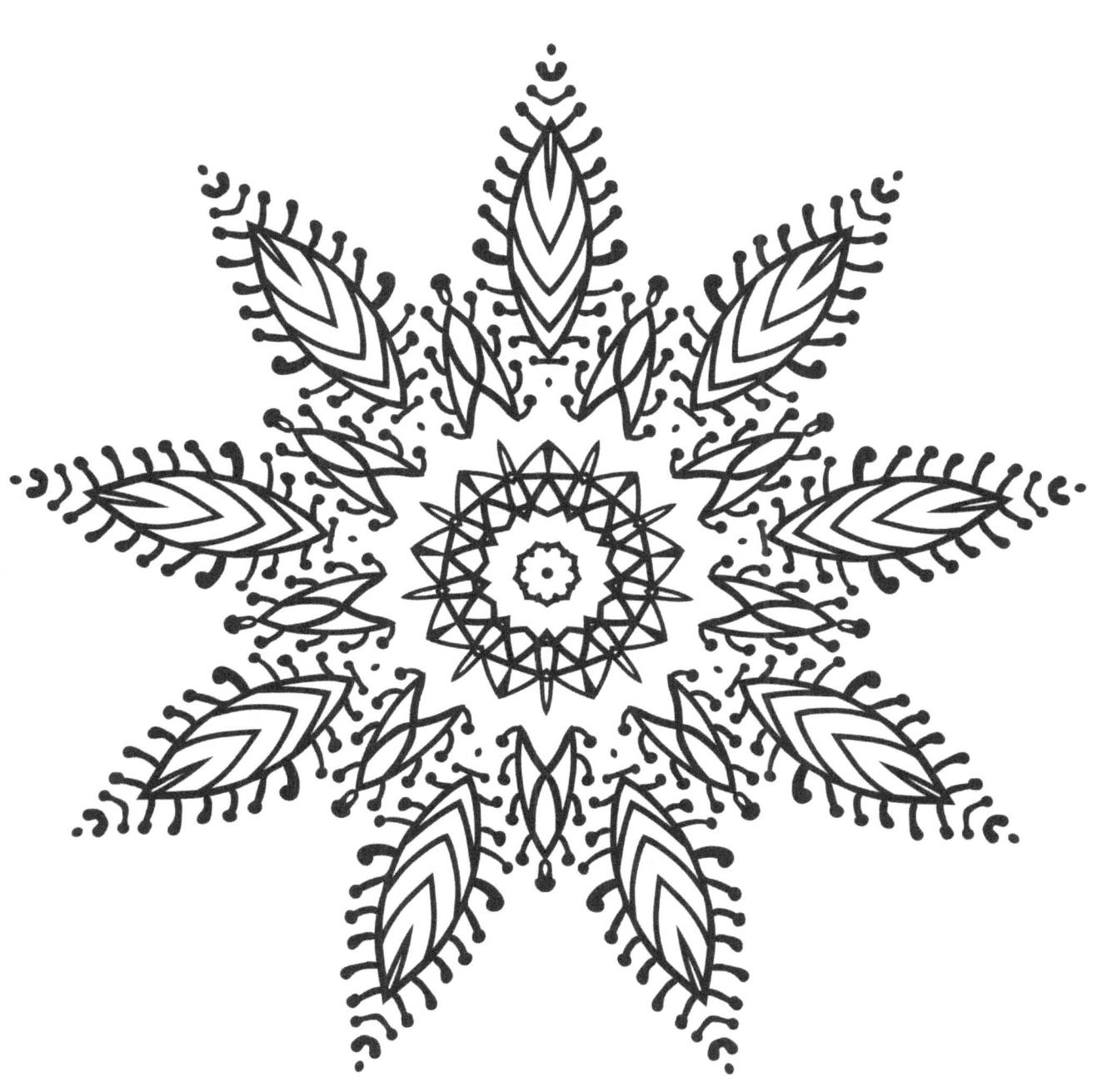

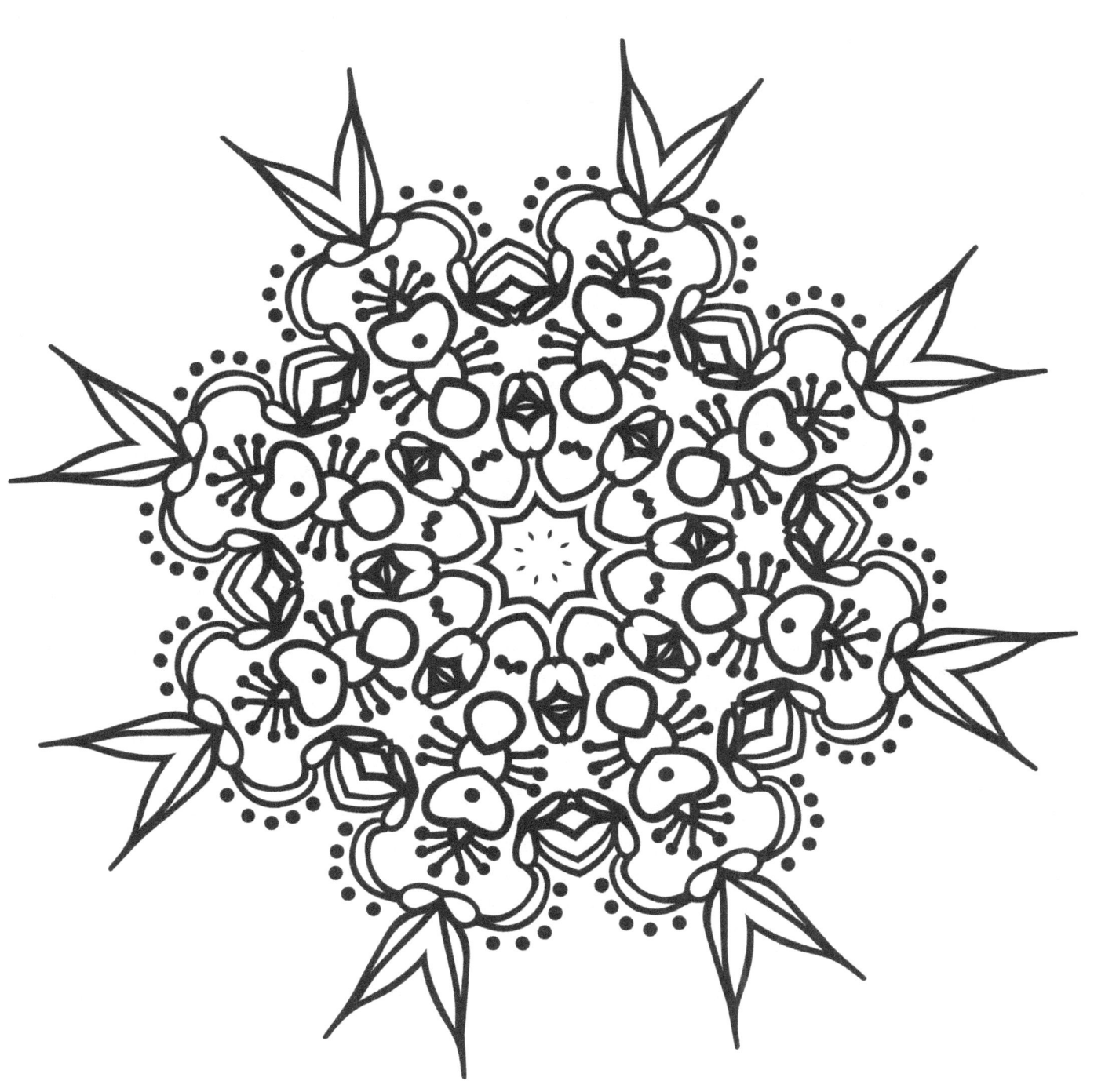

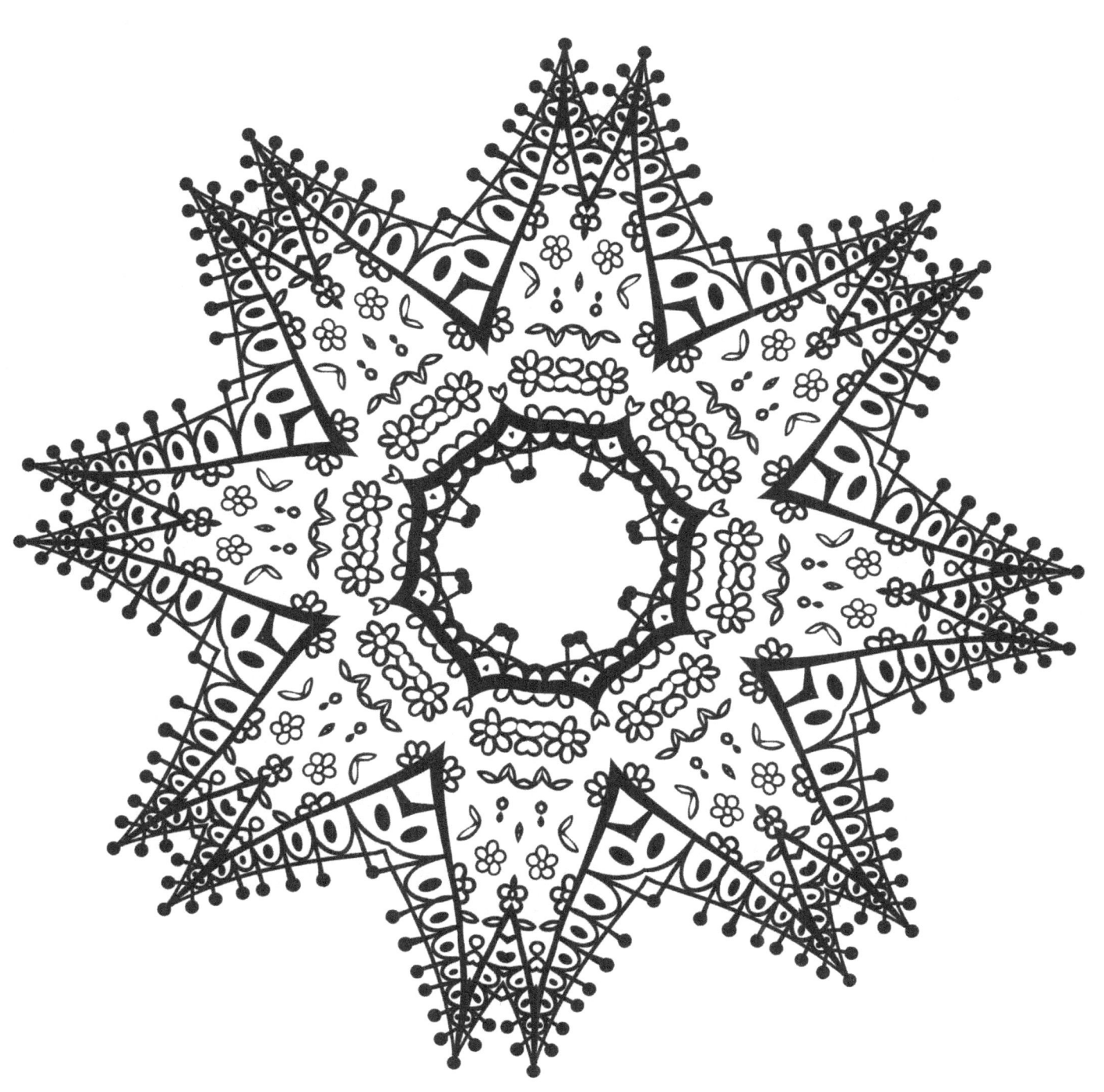

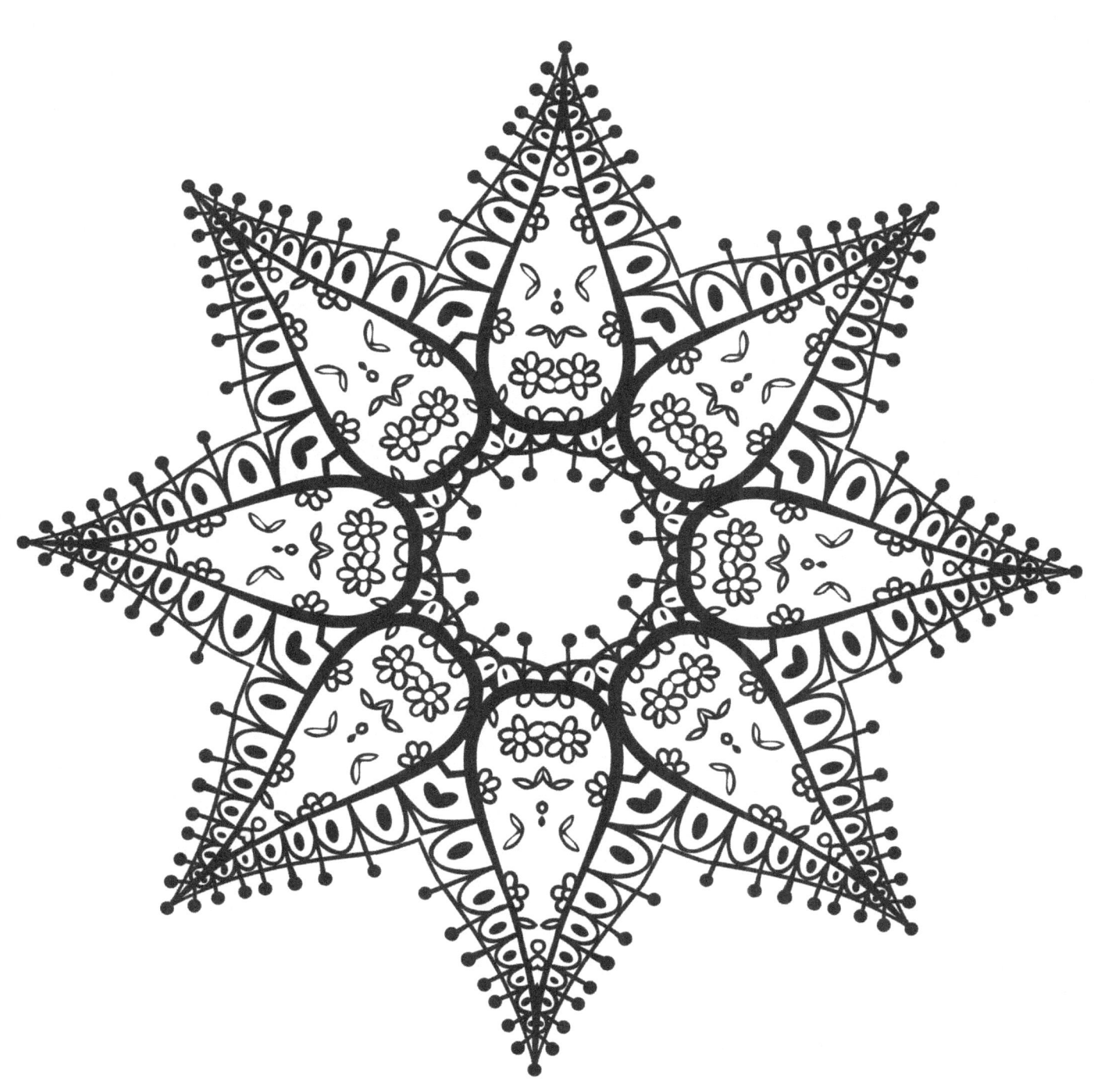

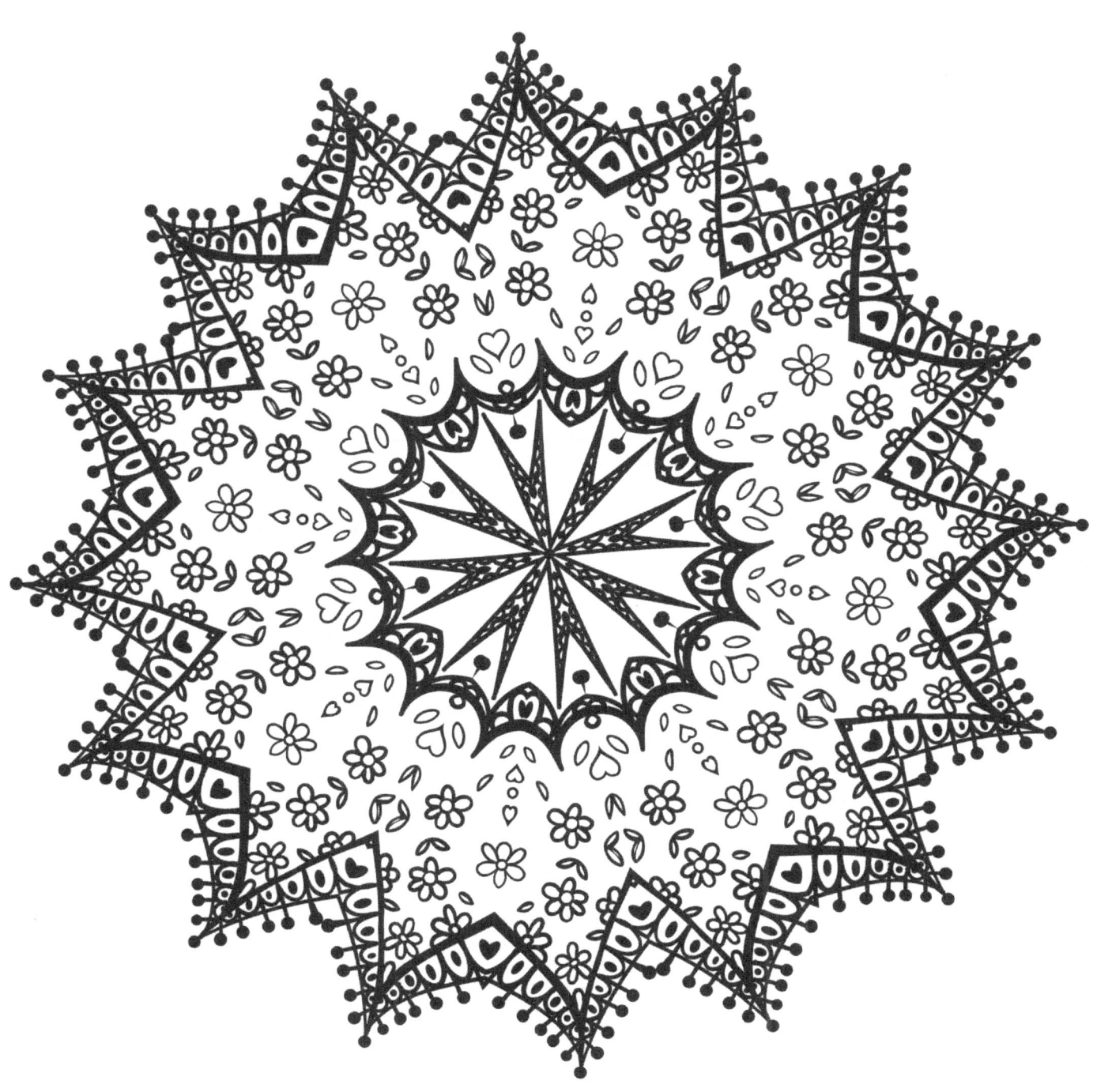

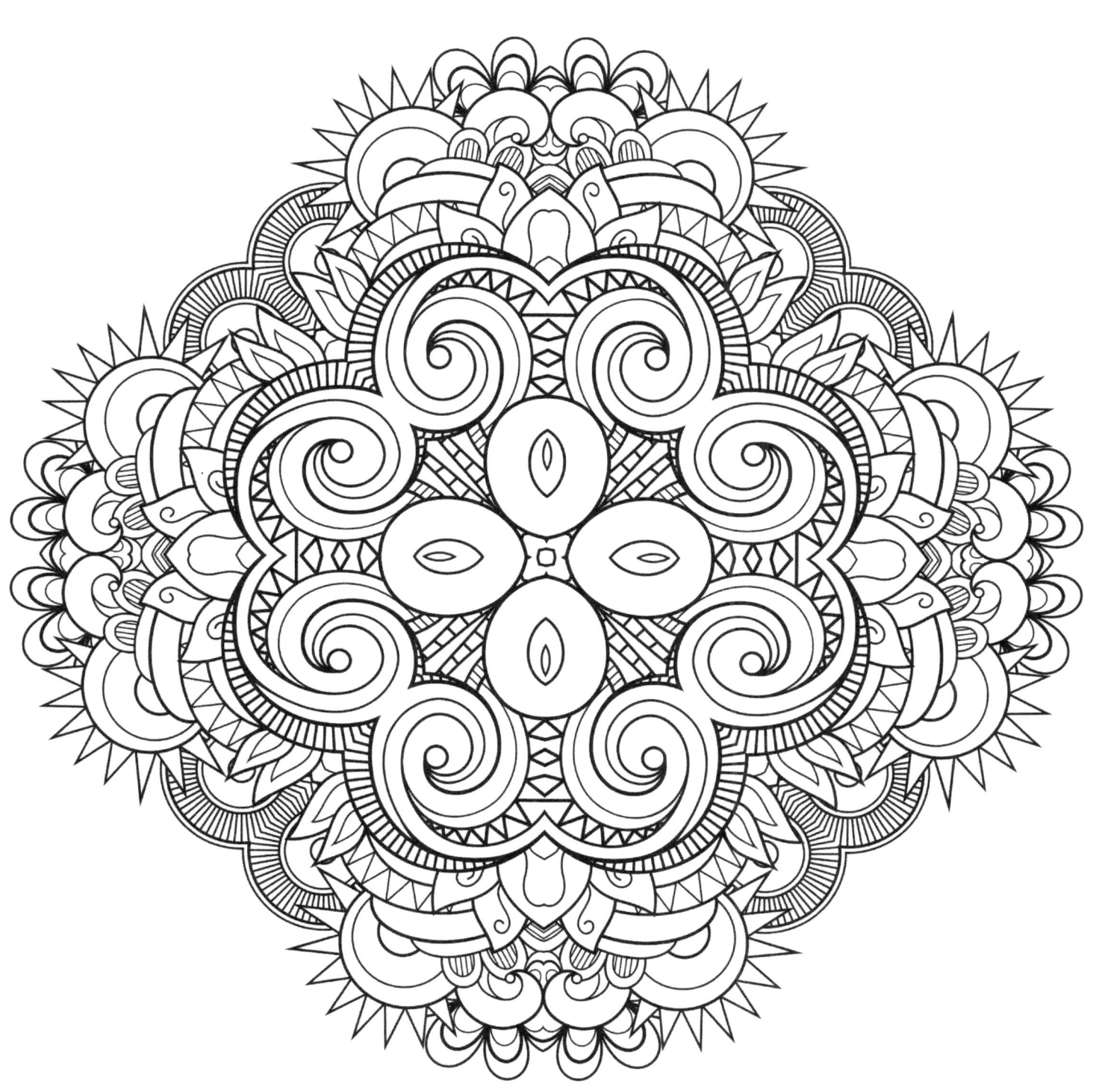

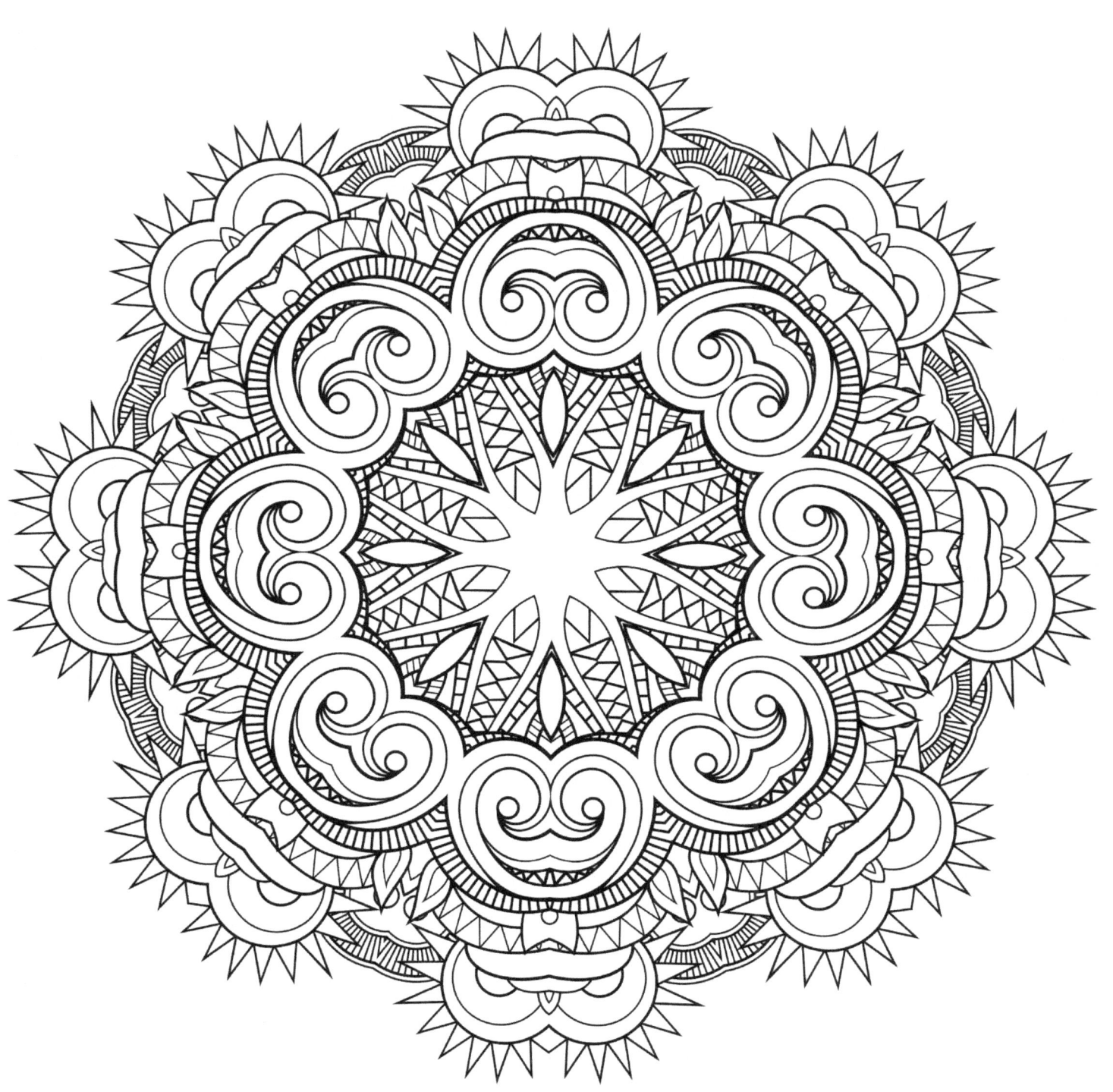

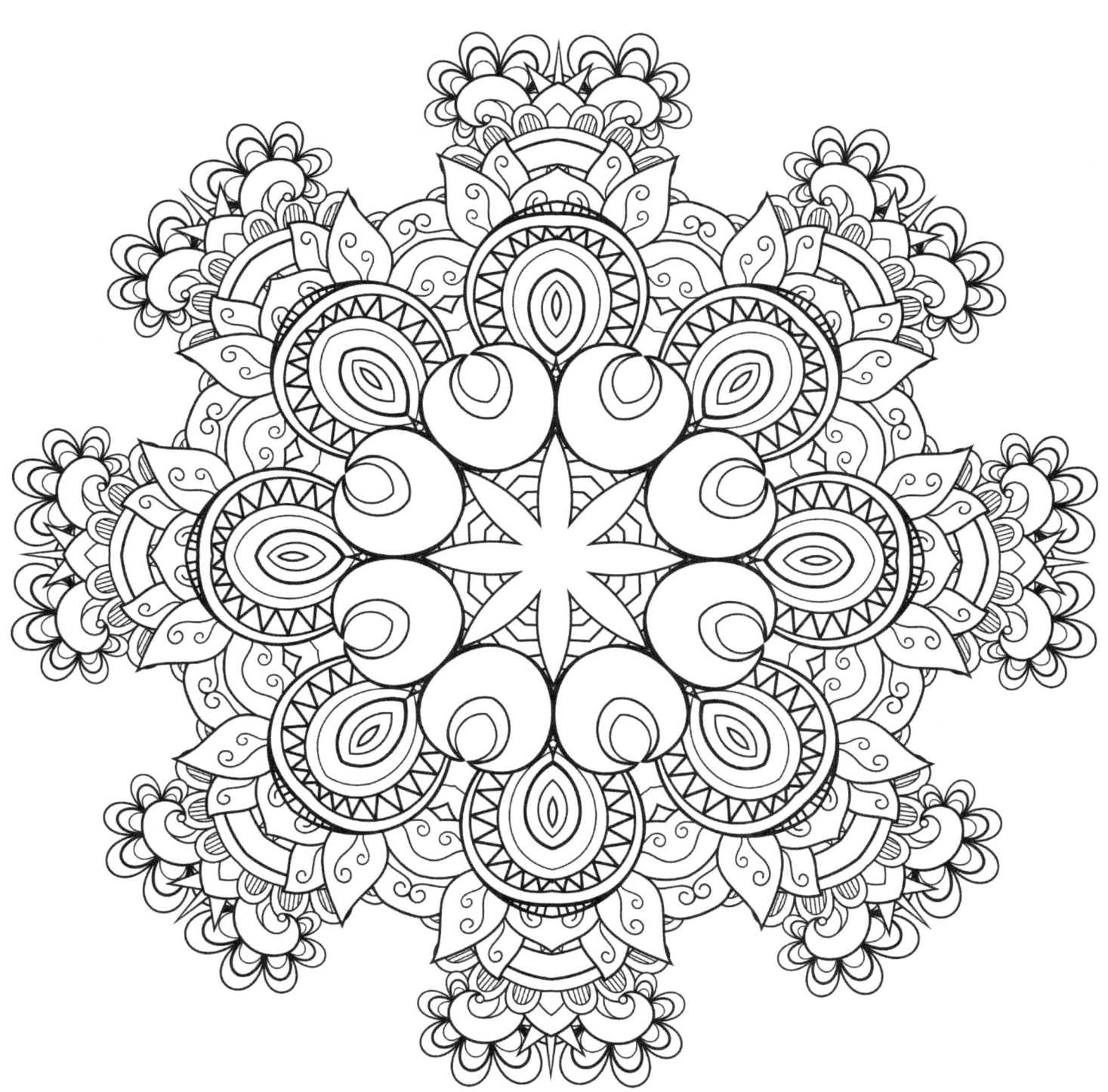

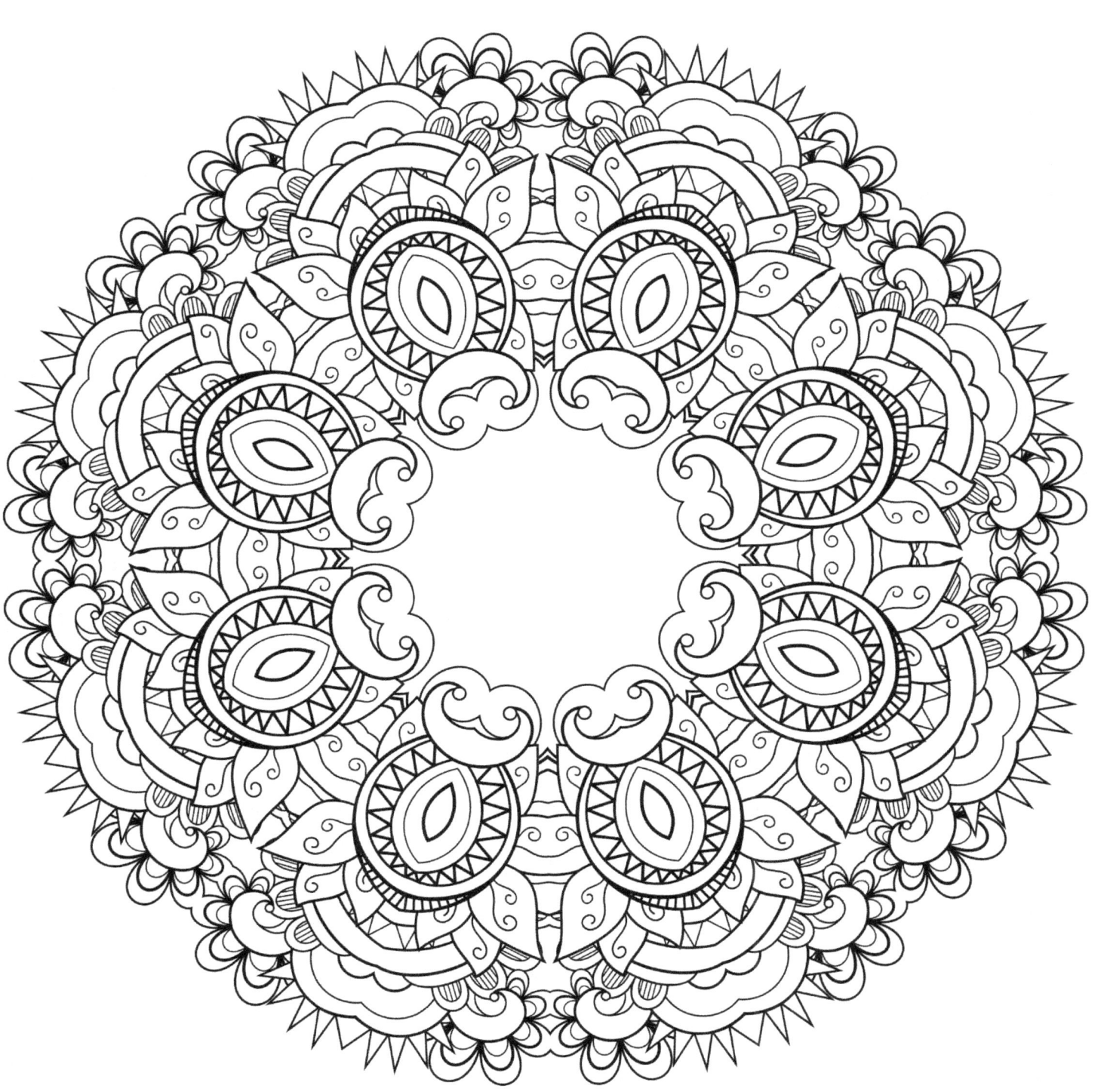

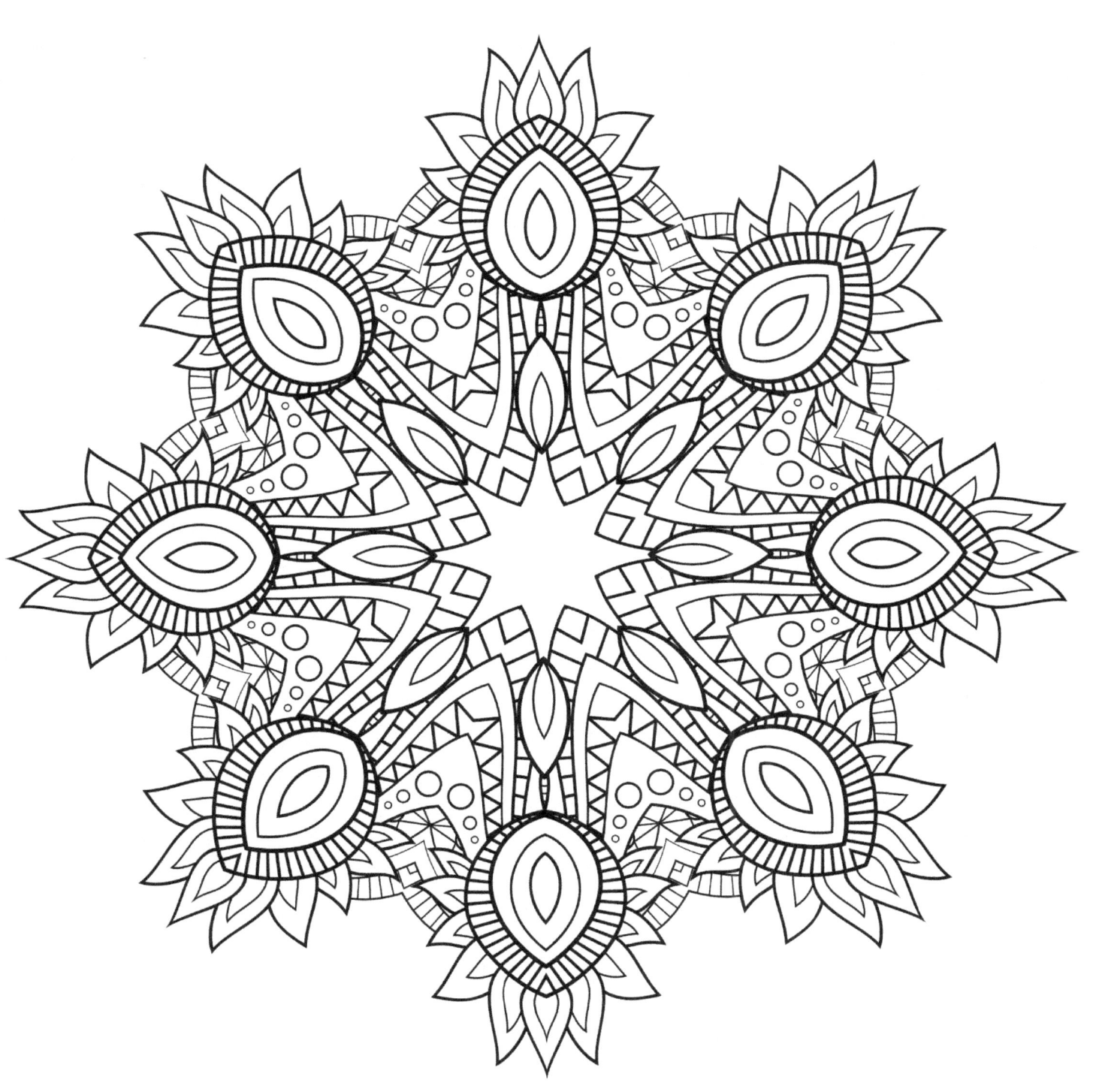

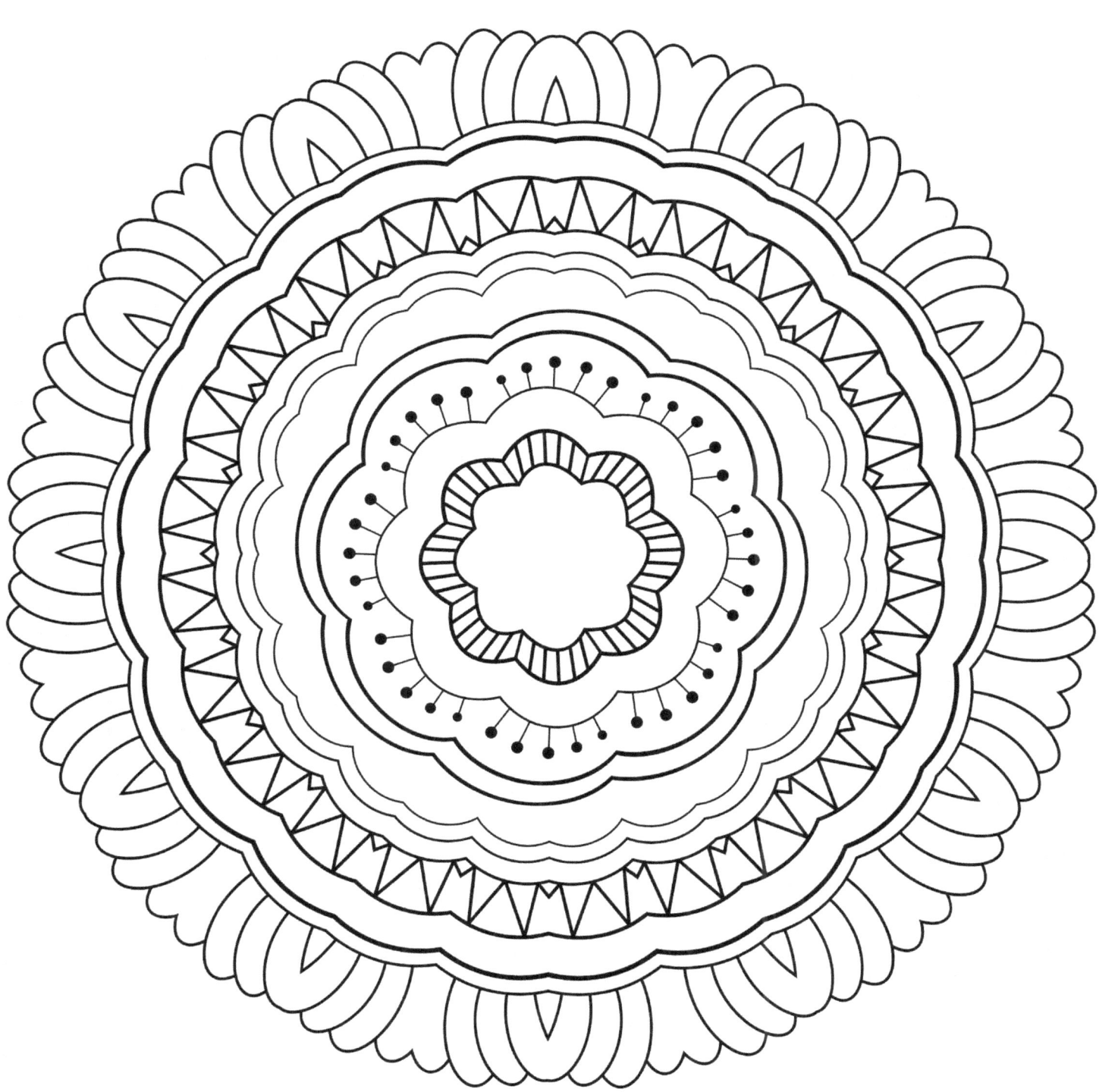

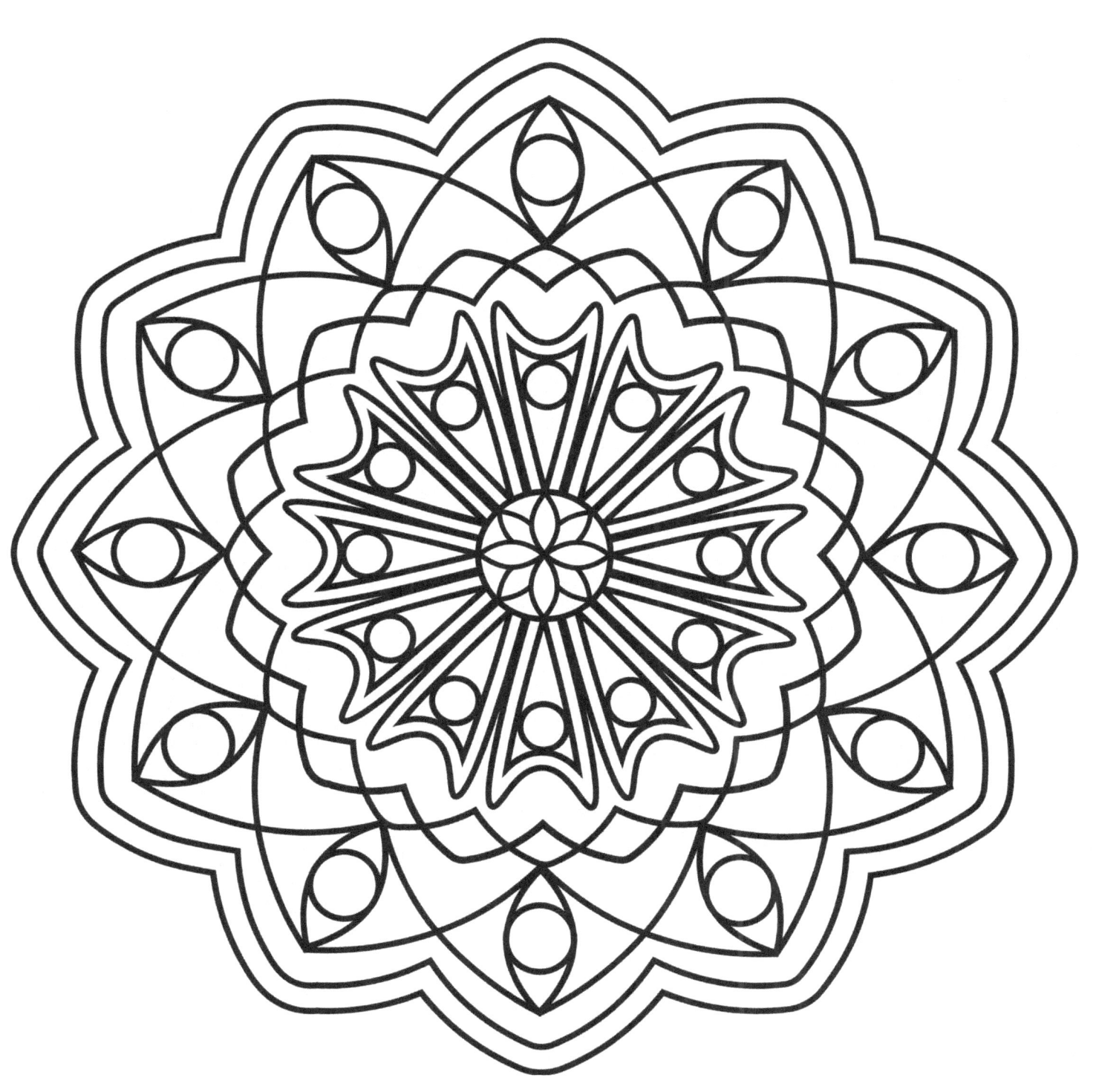

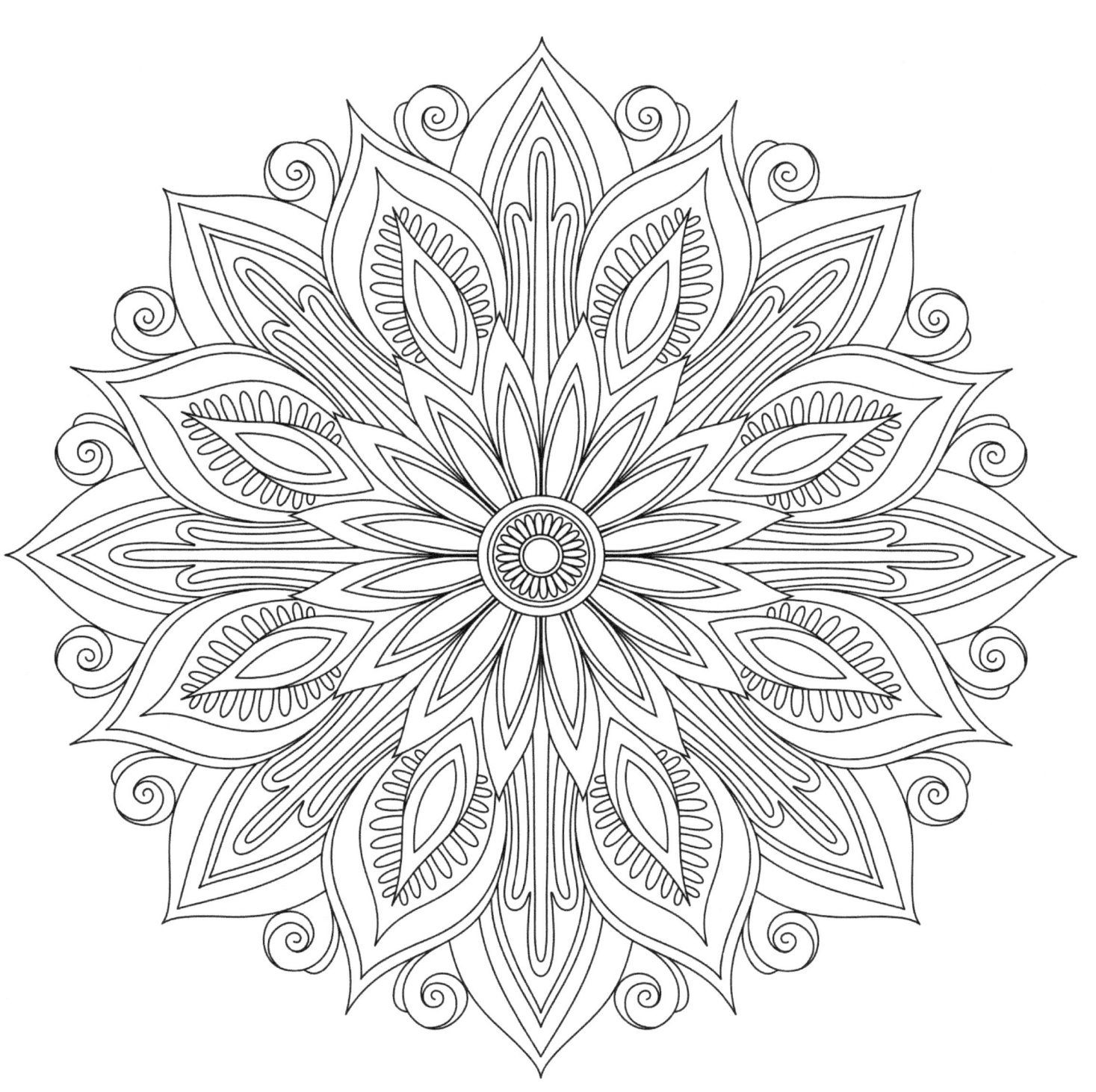

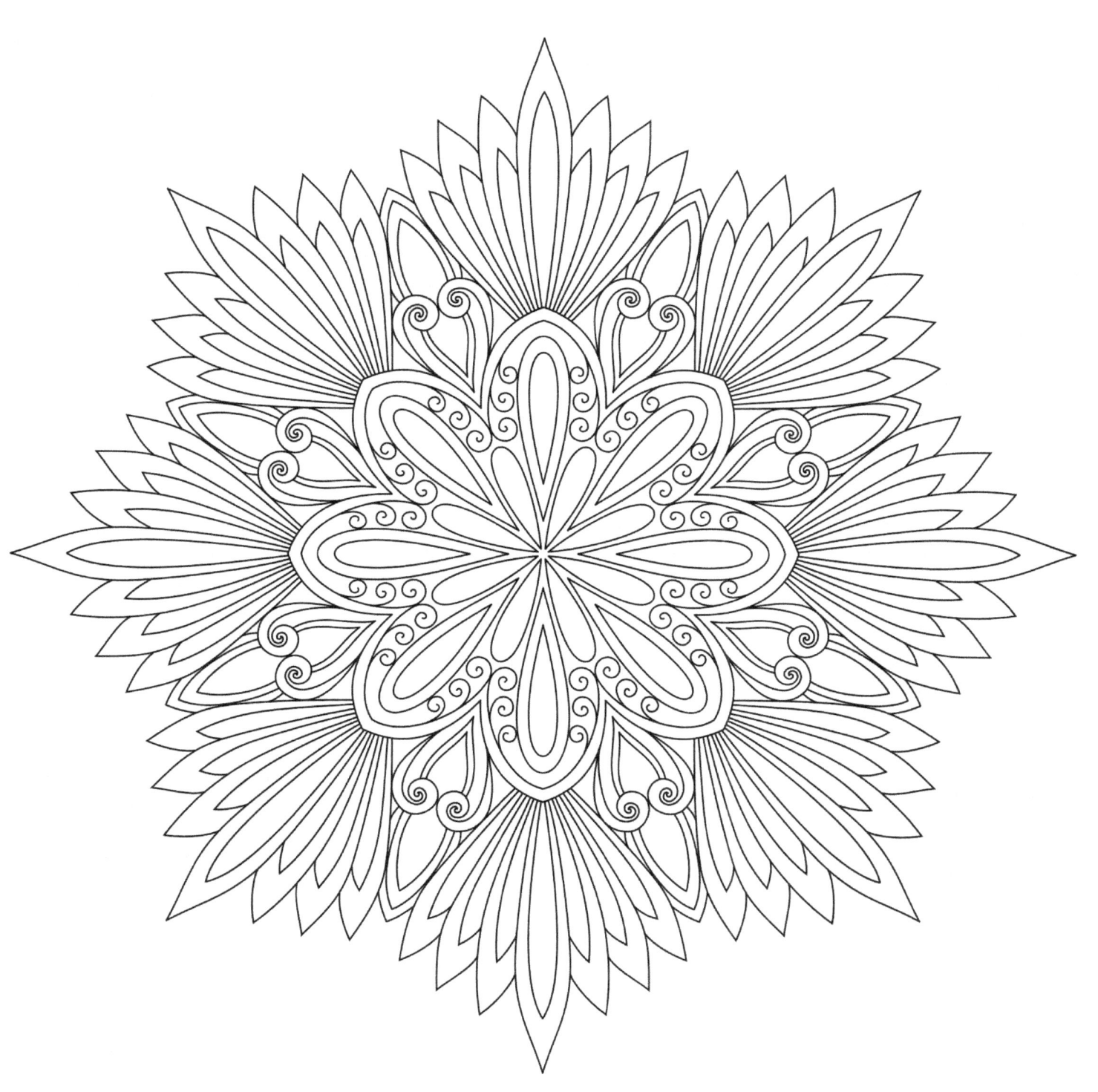

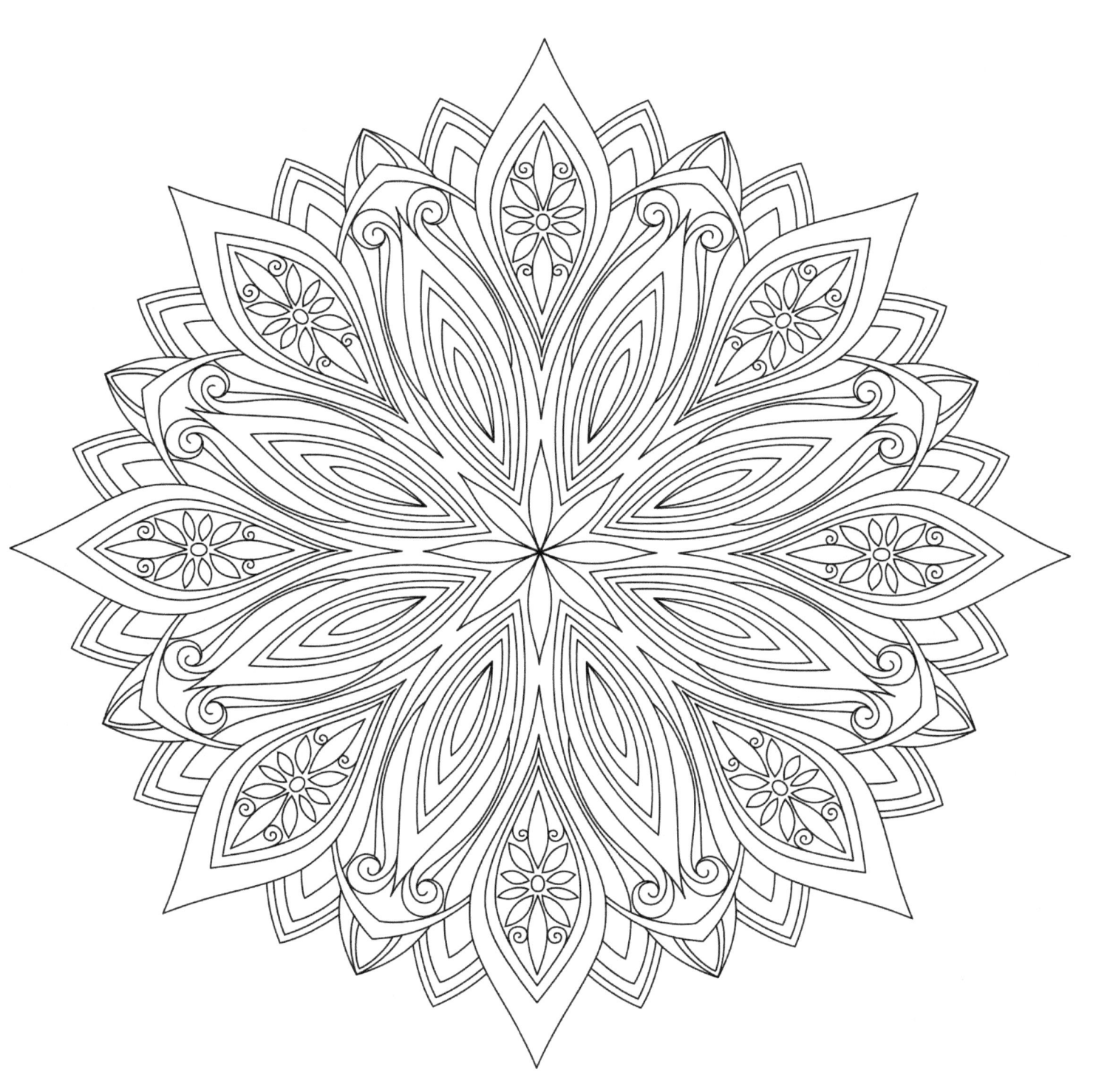

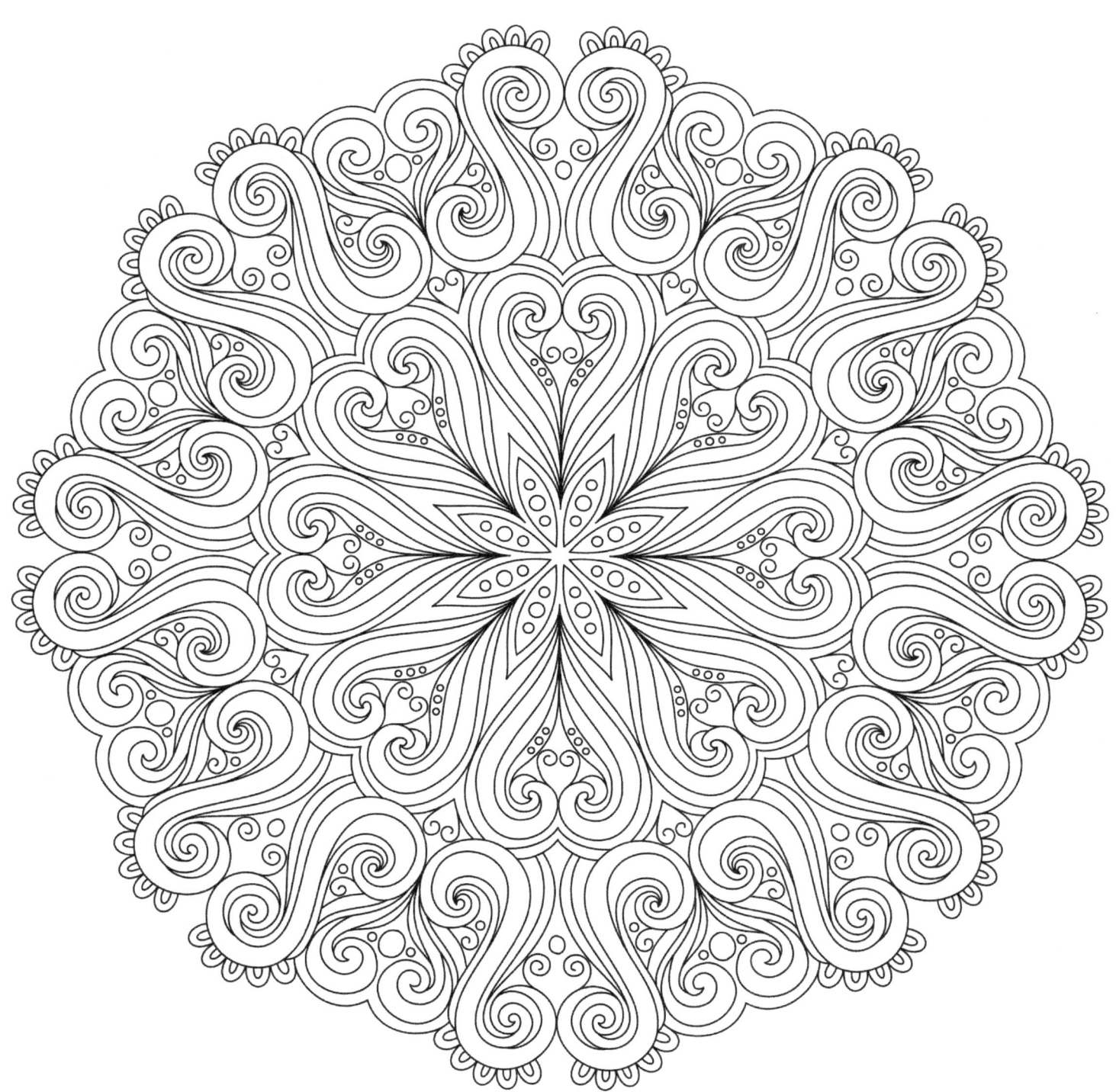

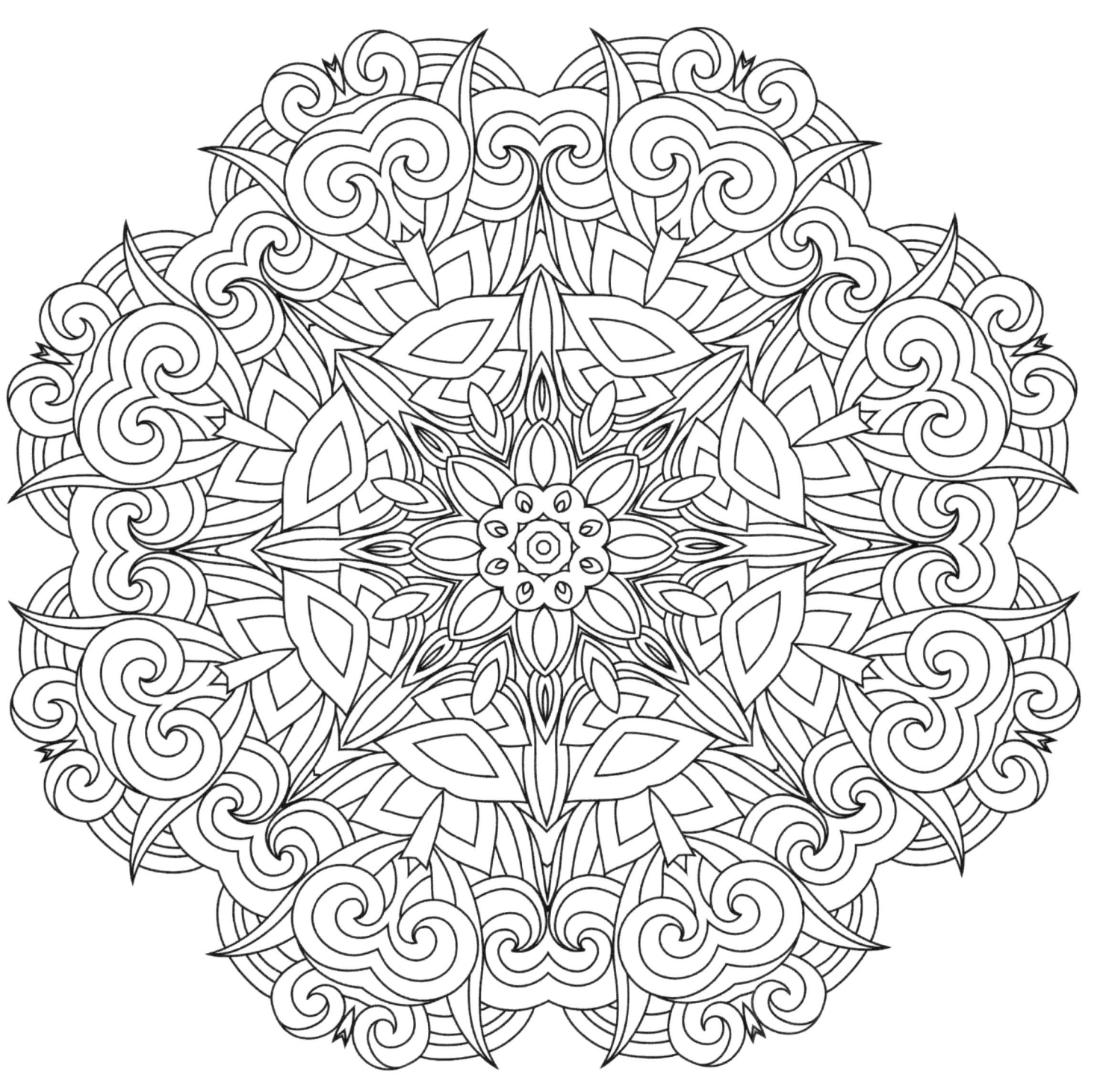

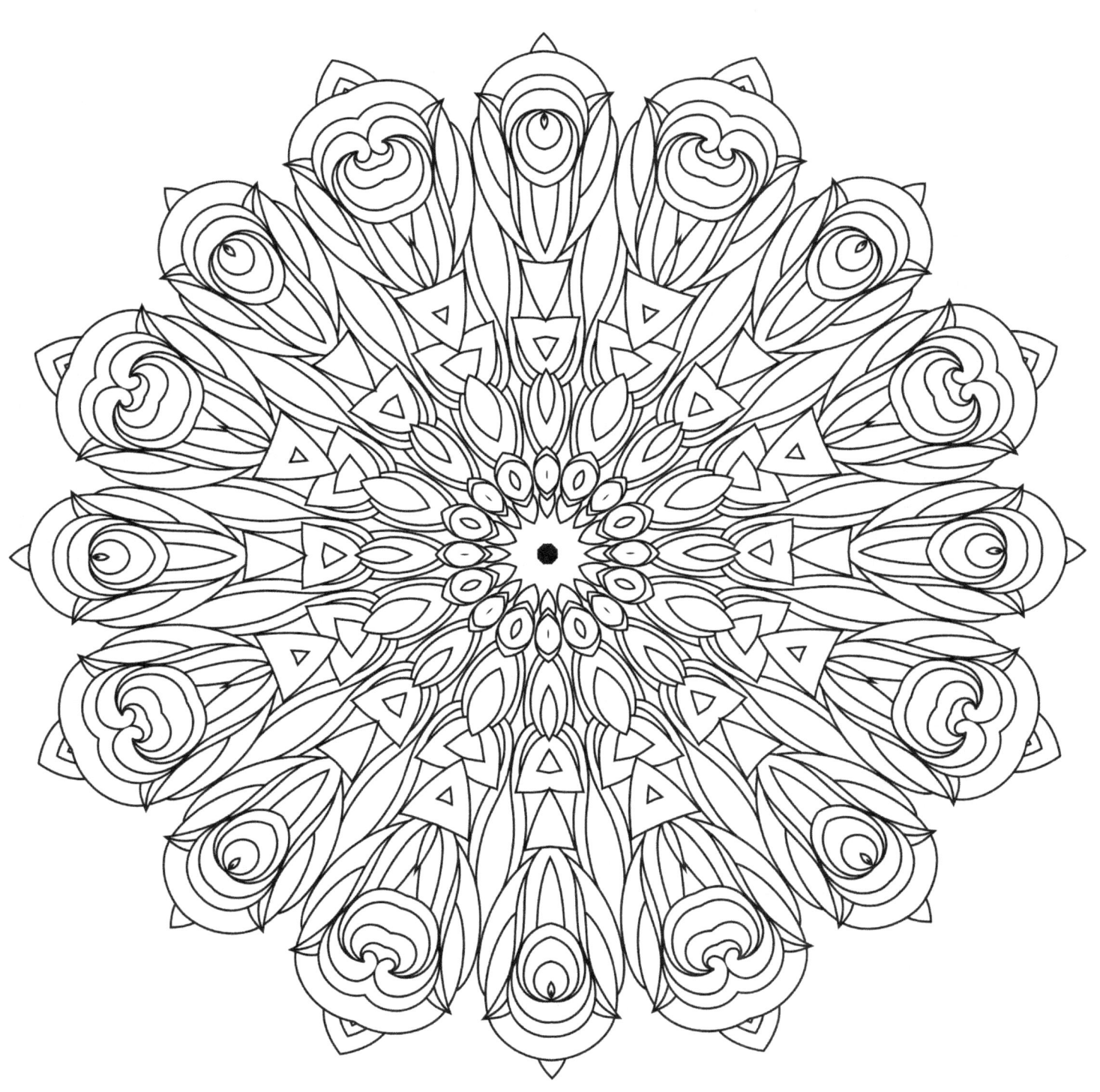

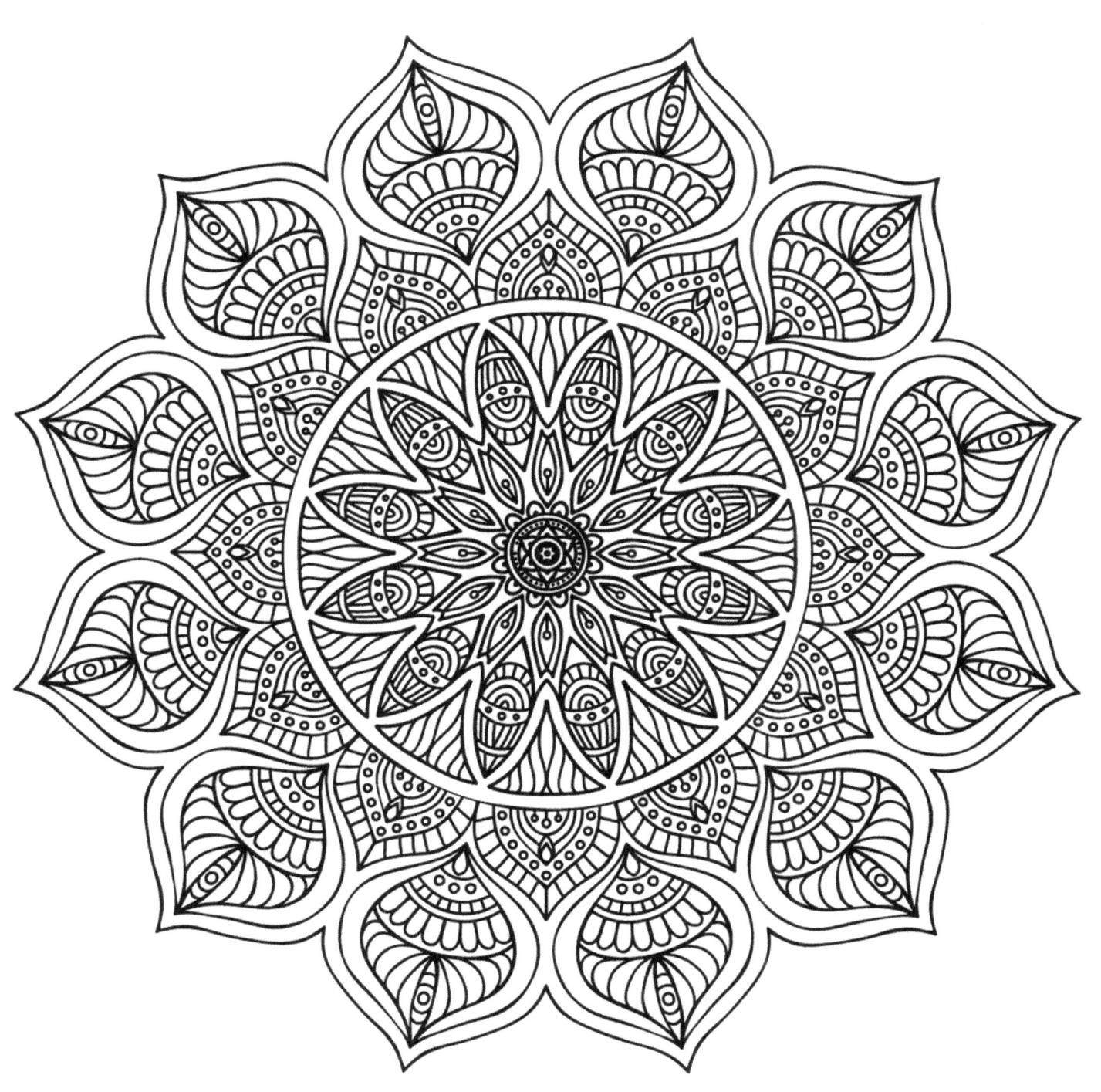

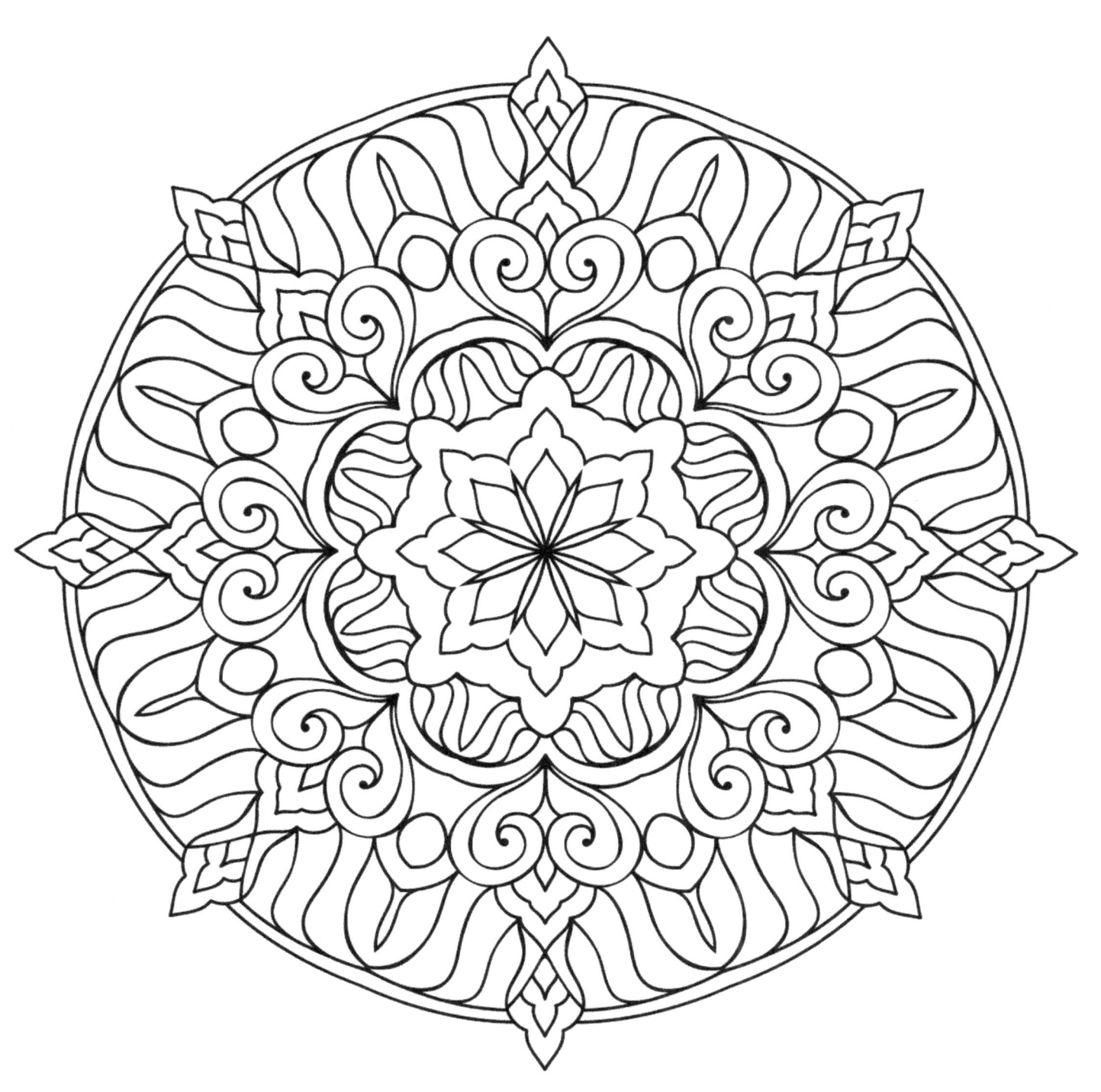

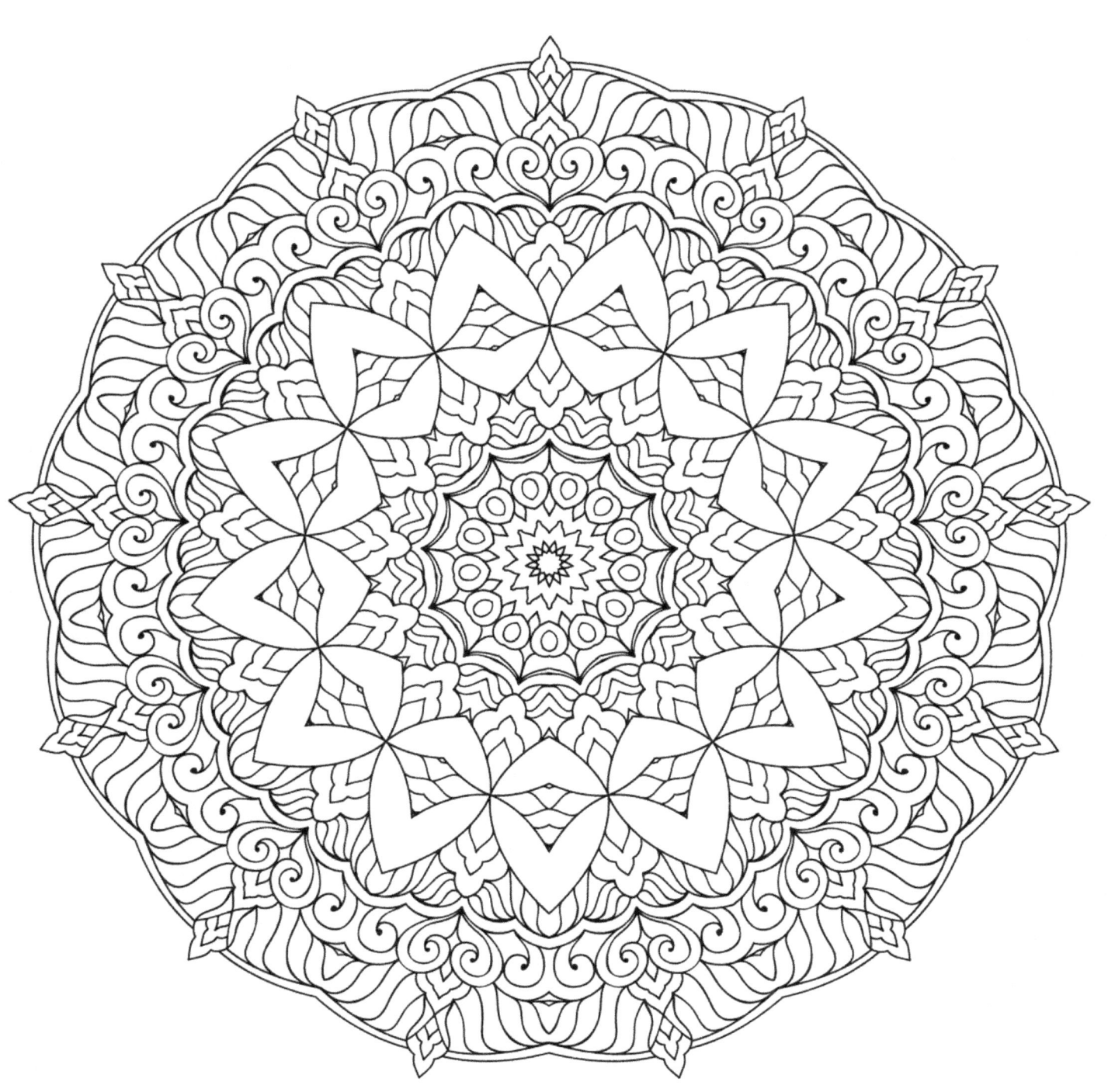

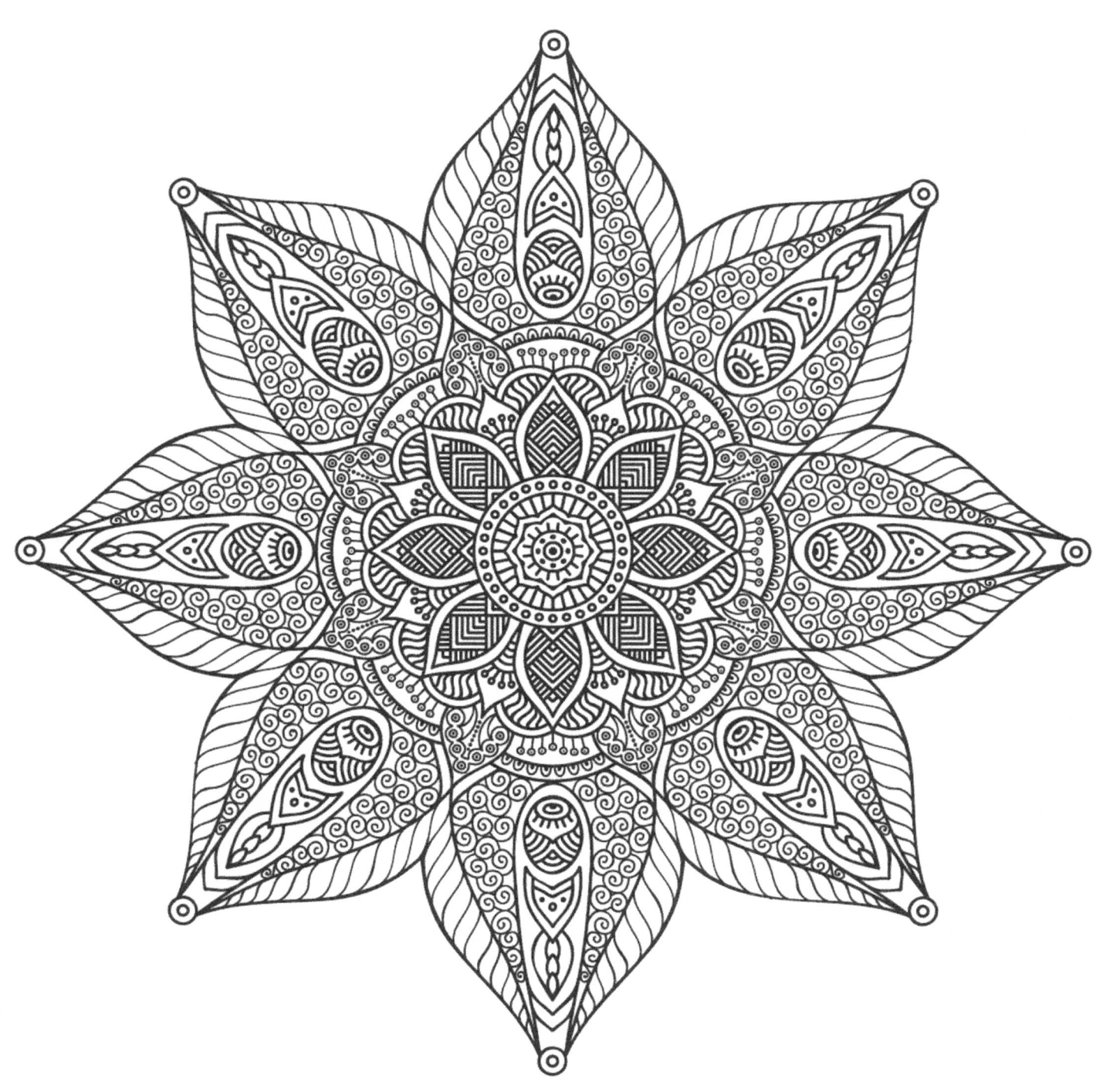

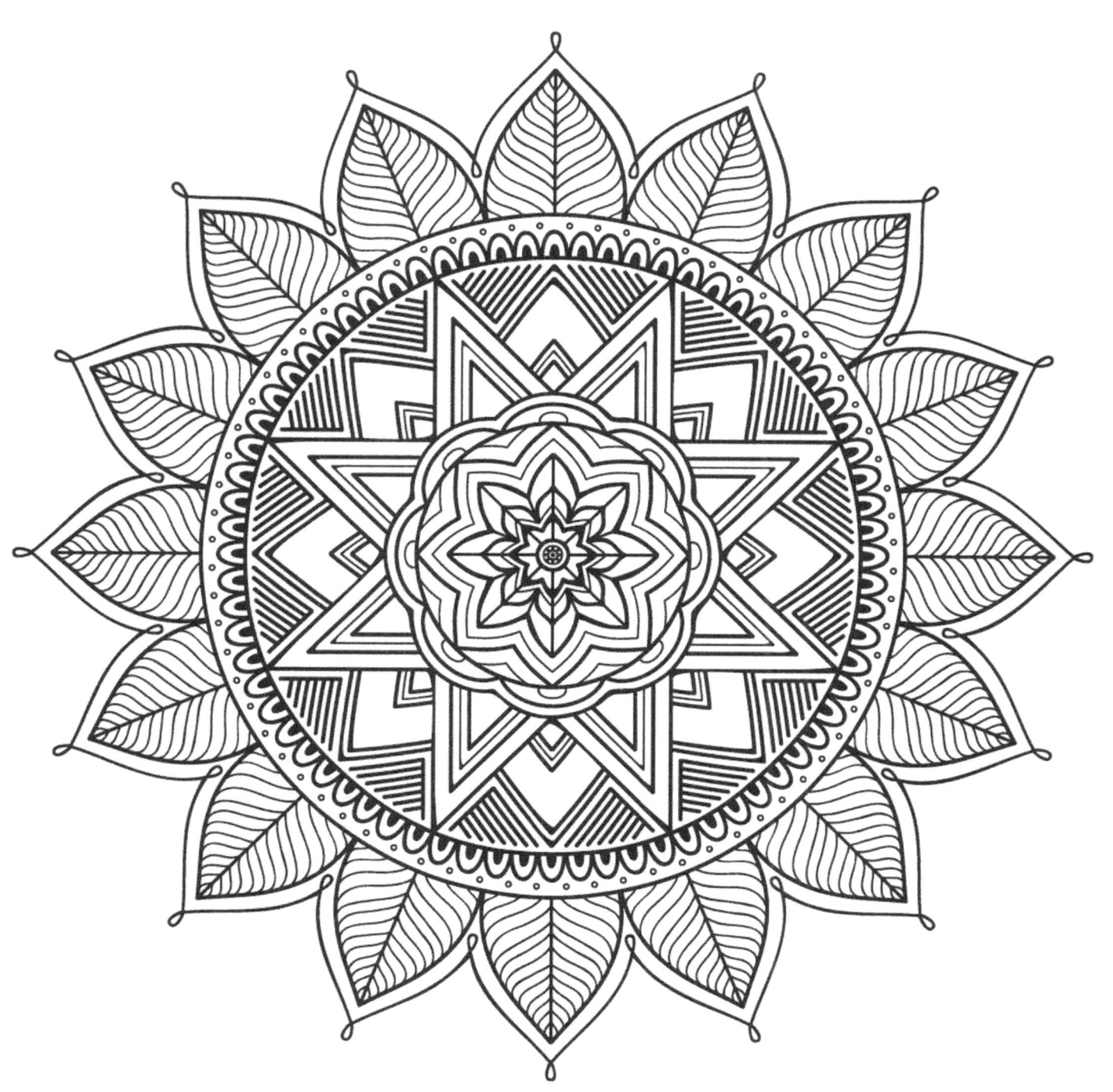

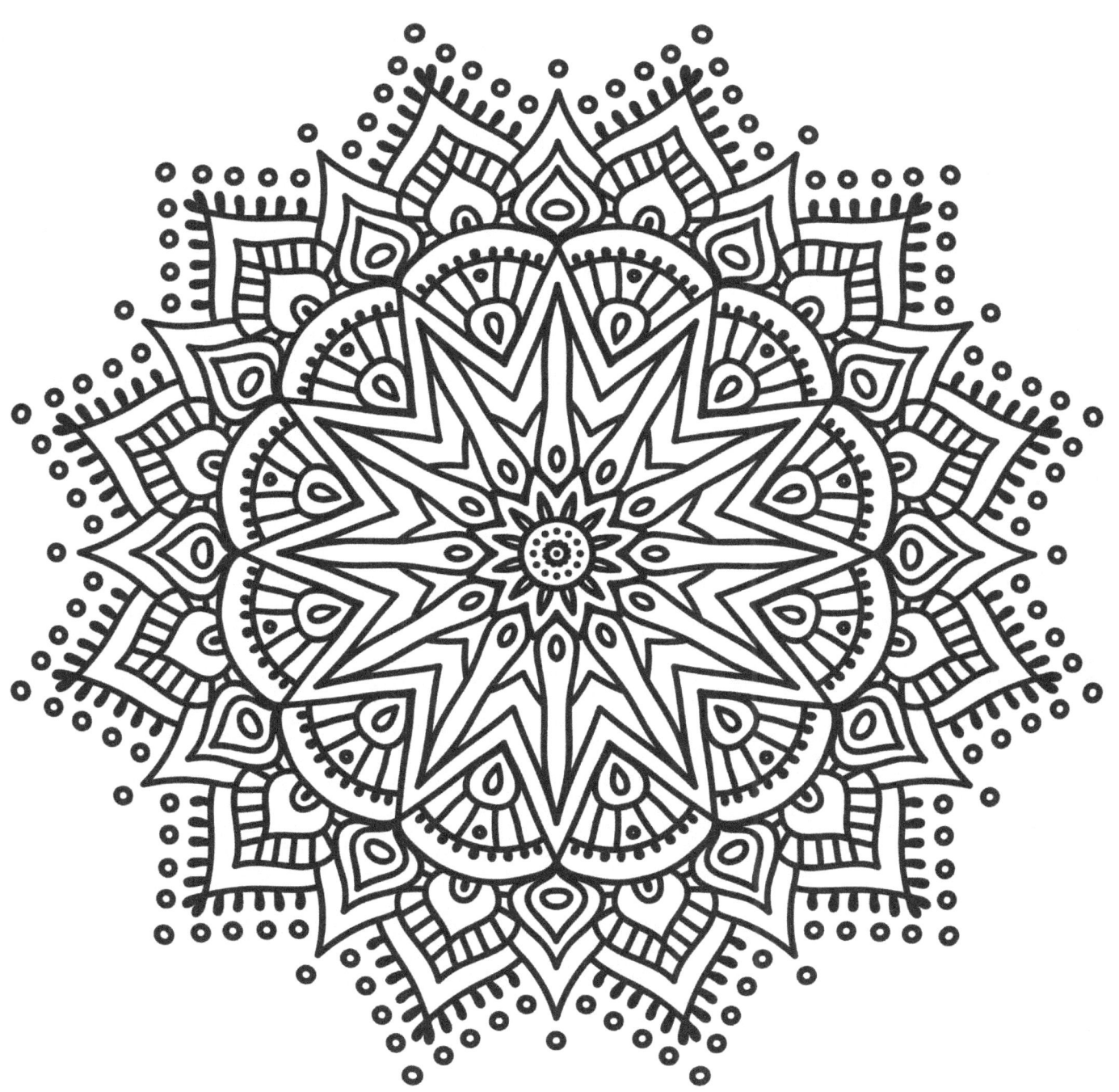

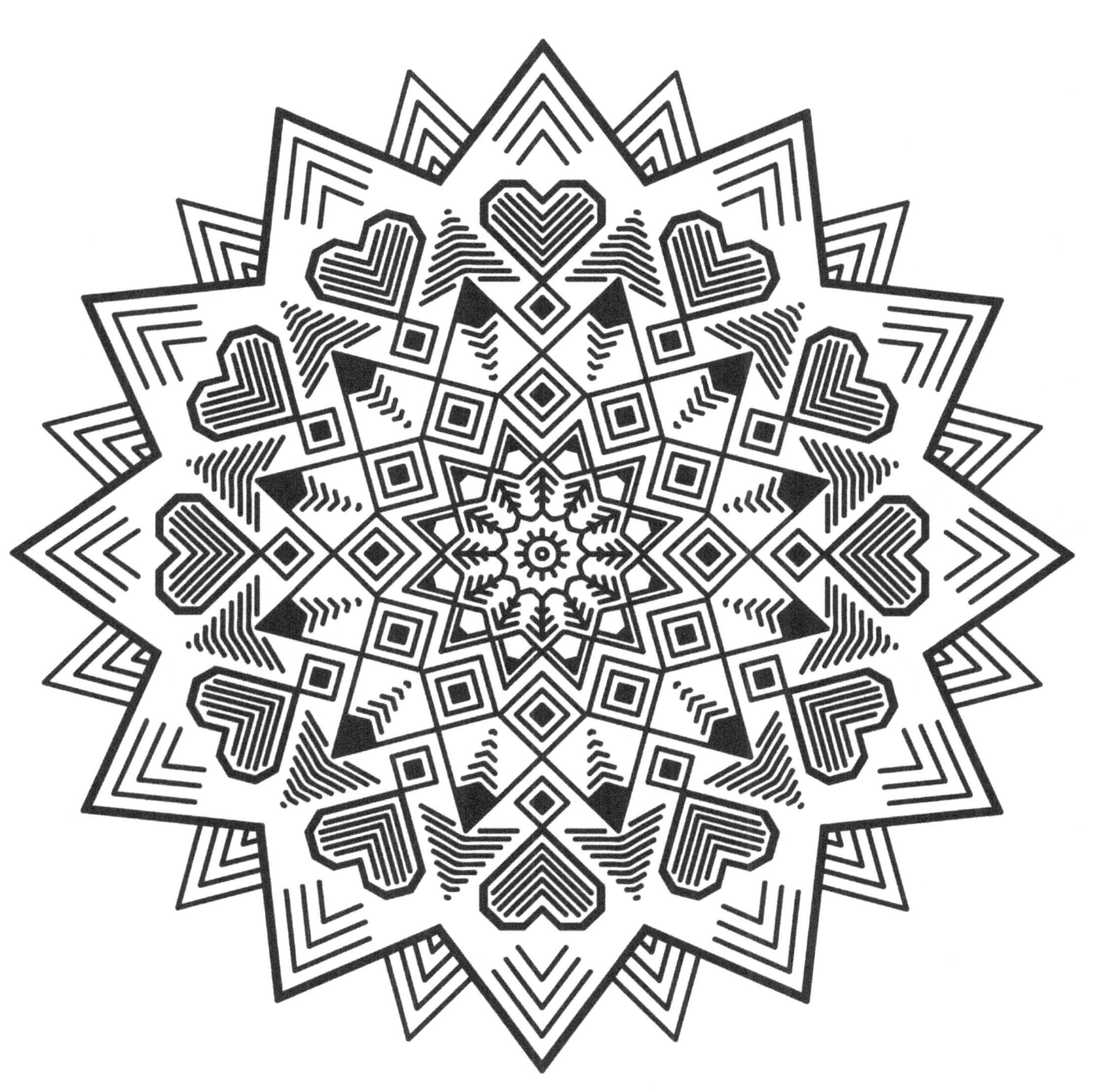

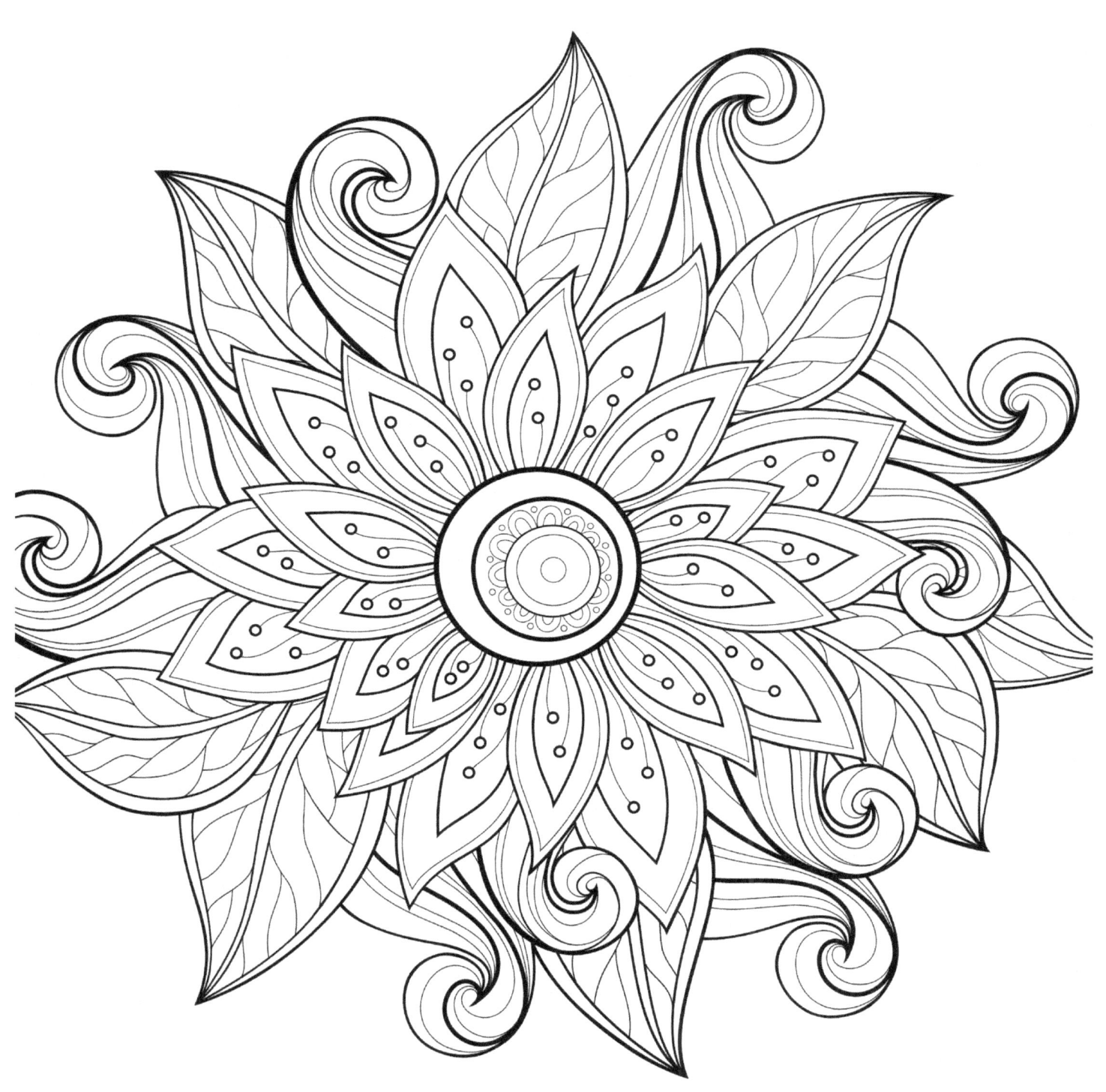